WISSENSCHAFTLICHE UNTERSUCHUNGEN
ZUM NEUEN TESTAMENT

2. REIHE

HERAUSGEGEBEN VON
MARTIN HENGEL · JOACHIM JEREMIAS · OTTO MICHEL

3

Salvation and Atonement
in the Qumran Scrolls

by

Paul Garnet

1977

J. C. B. MOHR (PAUL SIEBECK) TÜBINGEN

CIP-Kurztitelaufnahme der Deutschen Bibliothek

Garnet, Paul
Salvation and atonement in the Qumran scrolls. —
1. Aufl. — Tübingen: Mohr, 1977.
   (Wissenschaftliche Untersuchungen zum Neuen Testament: Reihe 2; 3)
   ISBN 3-16-140191-3
   ISSN 0340-9570

PREFACE

The present work is a revision of my 1971 Ph. D. dissertation in the Faculty of Religious Studies, McGill University, Montreal: *Atonement Ideas in the Qumran Scrolls*. It also incorporates material from my article, "Atonement Constructions in the Old Testament and the Qumran Scrolls."[1] Previous studies of Qumran soteriology have either concentrated on something other than atonement,[2] or have been studies of certain texts only.[3]

I am especially indebted to Professor George Johnston of McGill University, whose seminar introduced me to the serious study of the Scrolls and who directed the thesis on which this work is largely based. Thanks are also due to the staff of McGill Religious Studies Library for trouble taken in procuring books and material from other libraries. I am grateful to Dr. R.C. Culley, also of McGill, for his advice in connection with the approach to the problems of Qumran Hebrew syntax. I am also indebted to Abbé J. Starcky for taking the trouble to write out the text of the document 4QAhA and send it to me. It was through the good offices of Professor F.F. Bruce of Manchester that I was able to make contact with Abbé Starcky at that time. I would like to take this opportunity publicly to express my gratitude to Professor Bruce for the constant encouragement he has given me in my academic career since the time when I studied under him at Sheffield, and also for the inspiration provided by his

[1] *The Evangelical Quarterly*, 46 (1974), pp. 131-163. This material is copyright by the Paternoster Press and reproduced here by kind permission of the Managing Director, Mr. Jeremy H.L. Mudditt.

[2] E.g. Lucetta Mowry, *The Dead Sea Scrolls and the Early Church*, Chicago, 1962; A. Jaubert, *La notion d'alliance dans le judaïsme aux abords de l'ère chrétienne*, Paris, 1963, pp. 116-249; J. Becker, *Das Heil Gottes*, Göttingen, 1964, Pt. I.

[3] E.g. John V. Chamberlain, "Toward a Qumran Soteriology," *Novum Test.*, 3 (1959), pp. 305-313; W.H. Brownlee, "Anthropology and Soteriology in the Dead Sea Scrolls and in the New Testament," in *The Use of the Old Testament in the New and Other Essays*, ed. James M. Efird, Durham, N.C., 1972, pp. 210-240.

IV

own example as a Christian scholar.

Since the completion of the thesis, I have been indebted to those who have read it and given valued advice: Principal Matthew Black of St. Andrews, Professor E. Best of Glasgow, Dr. B.W.W. Dombrowski of Dalhousie and Professor Otto Betz of Tübingen. To Professor Martin Hengel and his fellow editors of the W.U.N.T. series I proffer my sincere thanks for their acceptance of this work into this series. Professor Hengel's patience and that of the house of Mohr during the time the final manuscript was being prepared are much appreciated.

For financial assistance in bringing the present work to fruition I am indebted to the Canada Council for the award of a Doctoral Fellowship during 1968-9 and of a Research Grant for 1972-3, as well as of a grant to cover thesis preparation costs. Thanks are also due to the C.A.S.A. agency of Concordia University, Montreal, for a grant towards the cost of publishing the final monograph.

I am grateful to my wife for help in checking the final drafts and to all my family for their forbearance during the time when I was "an exile in the desert".

Department of Theological Studies,   Paul Garnet
Concordia University,
Montreal.

December, 1976.

TABLE OF CONTENTS

ABBREVIATIONS

BASOR   *Bulletin of the American Schools of Oriental Research.*

BZAW   *Beihefte zur Zeitschrift für die alttestament-liche Wissenschaft.*

CJT   *Canadian Journal of Theology.*

NEB   New English Bible (1970).

NTS   *New Testament Studies.*

Rev. Bib. *Revue Biblique.*

Rev. Qum. *Revue de Qumran.*

RV   Revised Version.

TDNT I   *Theological Dictionary of the New Testament,*
             ed. by Gerhard Kittel, tr. and ed. by Geoffrey
             W. Bromiley (English translation of
(TWNT)   *Theologisches Wörterbuch zum Neuen Testament),*
             I, Grand Rapids, c. 1964.

TDNT V   *Ibid.,* ed. by Gerhard Friedrich, V, 1968.

Z. Theo. K. *Zeitschrift für Theologie und Kirche.*

c.   copyright

f 2 etc   fragment 2 etc.

INTRODUCTION

In his work on the teaching of Jesus, Joachim Jeremias
has asked,[1] "Is it conceivable that Jesus saw his death as
representative? Is that not clearly the doctrine of the
primitive community? The general currency in the world of
Jesus of ideas about the atoning power of death provides us
with an answer to the question." He then presents a summary
of these ideas, taken almost exlusively from rabbinical sources
and from II and IV Maccabees. The death of the righteous is
presented in this literature as "supererogatory suffering"
and that of the martyrs as a substitutionary atonement. He
concludes,

"This is the world in which Jesus lived. If he believed himself to be the messenger of God who was to bring God's final
message, and if he reckoned with the possibility of a violent
death, then he must have been concerned with the question of
the meaning and the atoning power of his death. So it is
hardly permissible to reject as untrustworthy from the start
the fact that the gospels claim that Jesus found the meaning
of his suffering outlined in Isa. 53, even if the material is
limited."

Whatever contact Jesus may have had with rabbinic Judaism,
or with the Hellenistic Judaism exemplified in II and IV Maccabees, it is probable that he had even closer contacts with
the non-rabbinic Palestinian Judaism often called "sectarian".[2]
It may seem strange that Jeremias adduced no witnesses from
this quarter apart from two references to apocalyptic literature which prove merely that "it could be said that martyr-
doms would usher in the end" (Ass. Mos. 9:7ff., Eth. Enoch
47:1-4). Now the Qumran scrolls are an important witness

---

[1] *New Testament Theology: the Proclamation of Jesus*, New York, c. 1971,
pp. 287f.

[2] The writer wishes he could find a better term, since this suggests
that rabbinic or Pharisaic Judaism was the "orthodox" or "main line"
position at this time. It also suggests that the men of Qumran constituted a "sect". If this is supposed to be a sociological term, it
is largely irrelevant to their soteriology. As a theological term it
unnecessarily suggests that the group was unorthodox. The present work
will call the group "the Community", their own self-designation.

to this sectarian Judaism, but Jeremias had already in 1965
denied the existence of any cogent evidence for the Isaianic
Servant Songs as an entity in the Community's consciousness
of its destiny.[1] The matter is by no means uncontroverted,
however. Matthew Black,[2] William H. Brownlee,[3] F.F. Bruce[4]
and A. Dupont-Sommer,[5] to name only a few, were convinced
that Qumran saw a Servant role either for itself or for its
leaders, whilst a more recent writer has envisaged a considerable emphasis on the Servant role, but only a minor
stress on atonement.[6] Clearly, there is still disagreement.

However important the Scrolls may be for New Testament research, they are also of interest as a religious phenomenon
in the history of Judaism. Possible relations have been
seen with Gnosticism, the Samaritans, the Karaites, the

----

[1]   *TDNT*, V, παῖς θεοῦ, p. 685.

[2]   *The Scrolls and Christian Origins*, New York, c. 1961, pp. 161-163.
The Dead Sea Scrolls and Christian Doctrine, London, 1966, pp. 12-18.

[3]   "The Cross of Christ in the Light of Ancient Scrolls," *The United
Presbyterian*, 111 (30.11.'53 - 28.12.'53); "The Servant of the Lord in
the Qumran Scrolls," *BASOR*, no. 132 (Dec. 1953), pp. 8-15 and no. 135
(Oct. 1954), pp. 33-38; "Messianic Motifs of Qumran and the New Testament,"
NTS, 3 (1956/7), pp. 12-30; *The Meaning of the Qumran Scrolls for the
Bible*, New York, 1964, pp. 138-143.

[4]   *Biblical Exegesis in the Qumran Texts*, Grand Rapids, 1959, pp. 50-58;
The New Testament Development of Old Testament Themes, Grand Rapids, c.
1968, pp. 91-94.

[5]   *Le Livre des Hymnes, découvert près de la Mer Morte (1QH)*, Paris,
1957, pp. 13-20; *The Essene Writings from Qumran*, tr. by G. Vermes,
Oxford, 1961, pp. 364-366.

[6]   " . . . suffering was directed towards the future, and was thought
to be productive of the new era. This would suggest that although the
image of the Servant was important for its aspect of suffering, the
aspect of atonement for sin was less central, or was thought to be merely preliminary to the creation of a new age." Barbara Thiering, "Suffering and asceticism at Qumran, as Illustrated in the Hodayot," *Rev. Qum.*,
8 (1974), p. 405.

Mandæans,[1] Zoroastrianism,[2] Pythagoreanism[3] and even with
Islam.[4] Since salvation doctrine is likely to prove an
important means of comparison between religions,[5] the
soteriology of Qumran is worth exploring quite apart from
any light it may shed upon the origin of early Christian doctrine.

The present study will examine the atonement ideas in the
Scrolls in the context of Qumran soteriology, since
atonement is a means of salvation. This material will be
approached through the Old Testament and the intertestamental
literature rather than through the New Testament, so as to
avoid "reading back" Christian ideas into the Scrolls. The
work takes into account all the major scrolls as well as the
more fragmentary documents published in *Discoveries in the
Judæan Desert*, volumes I, III and V.[6] The biblical manuscripts are excluded, since it is by no means clear that
conclusions about the theology of the Community can be de-
duced from any variant readings they may contain.[7] We plan

---

[1]   Helmer Ringgren, *The Faith of Qumran*, Philadelpia, c. 1963, pp. 250-
254.

[2]   Cf. e.g. 1QS 3:15-4:26 with the Gathic poem Yasna 30 (A.C. Bouquet,
Sacred Books of the World, London, 1954, p. 117). For further parallels
see Dupont-Sommer, "La 'Règle' de la Communauté de la Nouvelle Alliance,"
Revue de l'histoire des religions, 138 (1950), pp. 9f., but in this connection George Johnston has cautioned, "the sources of their doctrine are
far more biblical than Iranian" ("'Spirit' and 'Holy Spirit' in the
Qumran Literature," *New Testament Sidelights*, Hartford, 1960, pp. 30f.).

[3]   T.F. Glasson, *Greek Influence in Jewish Eschatology*, London, 1961,
ch. 8.

[4]   See C. Rabin, *Qumran Studies*, London, 1957, pp. 112-130.

[5]   See Mowry, *Op. cit.*, p. 6 and William Nicholls, "Liberation as a Religious Theme," *CJT*, 16 (1970), pp. 140-154.

[6]   Vol. I, D. Barthélemy and J.T. Milik, Oxford, 1955; vol. III, M. Baillet,
J.T. Milik and Roland de Vaux, 1962; vol. V, John M. Allegro, 1968.

[7]   So Ringgren, *op. cit.*, p. 1. The reading מחשתי in 1Q Isa[a] at Isa.
52:14, which is potentially of great theological importance, is not
borne out by 1Q Isa[b]. This removes any presupposition that the Community possessed a theologically nuanced "received text". The "inter-
pretative character" of 1Q Isa[a], noted by Brownlee (*The Meaning of the
Qumran Scrolls*, pp. 165-192), turns out to be a matter of clarification.
There is no sign of theological tendency.

to explore the Scrolls as far as possible in the chronological
order presented by J. Starcky.[1] Those documents which cannot
be dated with any degree of probability will be treated separately at the end. If Starcky's order shows signs of an
intelligible soteriological development, this will tend to
confirm his hypothesis. At least the tentative chronological
order offers the possibility of detecting whatever development there may be. Each Qumran document will be studied
separately and its purpose stated.[2] In so doing we shall be
uncovering its implicit soteriology and preparing the way to
see each relevant section in its proper context.

Throughout the present work the word "atone" will be used
in the sense which it has acquired from its employment to
render the verb כפר in the Old Testament. Its exact meaning
has been a matter of debate. In the Hebrew Bible this verb
can be followed by a variety of prepositions, or by no preposition at all, governing either the sins, the sinners or
the material objects for which "atonement" is made.[3] My
rendering "to atone for" covers all these cases and the
phrase "to make atonement" renders the absolute use of the
verb in Hebrew. Other translations of כפר are not excluded
by this. For instance, when God is the subject, "forgive"
is the more usual translation.

Something should be said regarding the Scrolls' date of
composition. In order to establish this, the probable date
of the writing of the manuscript copies must first be decided.
The opposite method, whereby the historical figures alluded
to are first identified,[4] has given rise to a great diversity

[1] "Les quatre étapes du messianisme à Qumran," _Rev. Bib._, 70 (1963),
pp. 481-505.

[2] On the methodological importance of studying each Qumran document by
itself in the light of its own central motif see B.W. Dombrowski, "The
Idea of God in 1Q Serek," _Rev. Qum._, 7 (1971), p. 515.

[3] For a discussion of these constructions in the Old Testament, see
Appendix B. For their use in the Qumran literature, see the relevant
sections in what follows. Both are discussed together in my "Atonement
Constructions in the Old Testament and the Qumran Scrolls."

[4] E.g. G.R. Driver, _The Judæan Scrolls_, New York, c. 1965.

of interpretations. It is too subjective. Objective tests
must be applied first and these are not one, but many.

The dates of the occupation of Khirbet Qumran as a religious
community centre have been established by Roland de Vaux.[1]

Ia - for a short time before Ib.
Ib - ca. 100 B.C. - 31 B.C.
II - ca. 1 B.C. - A.D. 68.

Studies of the size of the nearby cemetery,[2] of the types
of pottery,[3] of the ink[4] and of the handwriting[5] point
strongly to the conclusion that the Scrolls were written by
the people who were using the Community Centre, hence before
A.D. 68. The carbon-14 test,[6] the examination of the weaving
style of the cloth wrappings[7] and the type of jars in which

---

[1] *L'archéologie et les manuscrits de la Mer Morte*, London, 1961, pp.
1-37.

[2] *Ibid.*, pp. 45f.

[3] *Ibid.*, pp. 40-44.

[4] John M. Allegro, *The People of the Dead Sea Scrolls*, New York, 1958,
p. 137.

[5] De Vaux, *op. cit.*, p. 80.

[6] The carbon-14 test on the scroll wrappings initially "showed that the
flax from which the linen cloths were made was harvested in the year A.D.
33, with a margin of error of two hundred years either side of that
central date." (Allegro, *op. cit.*, p. 77) Driver objected that this
test was valueless, since logically any year within the period "is as
likely as the middle year." (*op. cit.*, p. 409) If this is the case,
one wonders why carbon-14 results alone should be singled out to defy the
laws of chance. Surely the "margin of error" is merely a way of expressing the level of confidence attaching to the result of the test in gen-
erally intelligible terms. The phrase corresponds statistically to one
standard deviation from the mean. This would imply that there would be
only a 32% chance of the flax having been gathered outside the period
168 B.C. - A.D. 233 (see e.g. M.J. Moroney, *Facts from Figures*, 2nd ed.,
London 1953, p. 63). The half-life of carbon-14 has now been revised
and these figures have to be altered, the middle figure to 20 B.C. and
the outside limits to 220 B.C. - A.D. 180 (Menahem Mansoor, *The Dead Sea
Scrolls*, Grand Rapids, 1964, p. 25). On this basis, the probability of
the flax having been harvested in time to have been used to wrap a scroll
before A.D. 68 would be about 65%. The carbon-14 evidence is not over-
whelming, but it must be allowed to make its contribution to the discussion.

[7] G.M. Crowfoot, "The Linen Textiles," *Discoveries*, I, pp. 22, 24, 27.

some of the Scrolls were found,[1] all point to a first-
century date of deposit for the Scrolls, probably some
time before A.D. 68.

As for the date of the writing of the actual manuscripts,
the temperature test on the leather on which they were written,[2] as well as the palæographical[3] and orthographical[4]
findings, indicate dates for the individual scrolls ranging
from ca. 175 B.C. - A.D. 50.

Starcky's dating of the original compositions takes into
consideration the probable dates of the surviving copies
which have been established by the objective criteria we have
just reviewed. Within this framework Starcky has enunciated
a dating hypothesis based on the messianic ideas contained
in each document. We propose to use this hypothesis as our
framework.[5]

It remains to consider the chronology of 1QH so as to justify the division of this scroll which we are to follow in
chapters I and II. The scroll of the *Thanksgiving Hymns* is
not very well preserved. Though much of the earlier columns
remains intact, sizable lacunæ appear in columns 5-11 in the
middle of the lines from about line 15 to line 30. Columns
12-18 are even more fragmentary. Furthermore, the beginnings
and endings of all the columns are heavily eroded. In spite
of the ravages of time, it is still possible in most cases to
delimit individual hymns by means of the opening words of
thanks.   Both Dupont-Sommer and J. Licht have divided the
text into individual hymns and there is very substantial

---

[1] Millar Burrows, *The Dead Sea Scrolls*, New York, 1955, p. 80; de Vaux,
op. cit., pp. 78f.

[2] De Vaux, *op. cit.*, pp. 76f.

[3] P. Wernberg-Møller, *The Manual of Discipline*, Leiden, 1957, pp. 1ff;
de Vaux, *op. cit.*, pp. 76, 87; Burrows, *op. cit.*, p. 87; see too J.C.
Trever, "1Q Dan[a], the Latest of the Qumran Manuscripts," *Rev. Qum.*,
7 (1970/1), pp. 277-286.

[4] Wernberg-Møller, *op. cit.*, p. 6.

[5] *Vid. supra*, pp. 3f.

agreement between them.[1]

The hymns can be divided into groups according to the probable identity of the worshipper who is speaking in them:-

1. the founder of the Community,[2]

2. a leader of the Community,[3]

3. a member of the Community.[4]

---

[1] See the respective divisions as set out by M. Mansoor, *The Thanksgiving Hymns*, Grand Rapids, 1961, pp. 33f. In the present essay the individual hymns will be referred to by a number (Licht's) followed by a letter (Dupont-Sommer's):-

1	A	1:1-39	10	J	5:20-39	19	R	10:14-11:2	28	A^1 16:3-19
2	B	2:5-19	11	J	6:3-36	20	S	11:3-14	29	B^1 17:1-8
3	C	2:20-30	12	K	7:1-5	21	T	11:15-34	29	C^1 17:9-15
4	D	2:31-38	13	L	7:6-25	22	U	12:2-35	30	D^1 17:17-25
5	E	3:5-18	14	M	7:26-33	23	V	13:1-20	31	E^1 17:26-27
6	F	3:19-36	15	N	7:34-8:3	24	W	14:1-7	32	F^1 18:1-31
7	G	3:37-4:4	16	O	8:4-37	25	X	14:8-22		
8	H	4:5-5:4	17	P	9:3-36	26	Y	14:23-27		
9	I	5:5-19	18	Q	9:36-10:12	27	Z	15:9-26		

Of the above, 29 B^1 is too fragmentary to assign to a probable author or to assess its soteriological contents in any way, whilst 16 O and 17 P are judged by the present writer to constitute one hymn only, since the beginning of col. 9 reads like a continuation of the end of col. 8.

[2] The criteria by which these may be distinguished have been summarized by Becker, *op. cit.*, p. 51: "Das Hauptmerkmal ist dabei die Struktur des Ichs der Psalmen. Ein weiteres typisches Zeichen sind Aussagen über Feinde und Nöte, die auf eine einmalige historische Situation schliessen lassen und im Zusammenhang mit dem genannten exzeptionellen Ich stehen. Ebenso charakteristisch sind solche Aussagen, bei denen das Ich davon spricht, dass es die Gemeinde gegründet habe und ihr vorstehe."

The author of these hymns would probably be the same person as the "Teacher of Righteousness" of CD, but not necessarily the same as the figure bearing that title in 1QpHab, since the possibility should not be ignored that this title was given to a succession of the community leaders (*vid.* M. Black, *The Dead Sea Scrolls and Christian Doctrine*, pp. 9f.). In view of CD 1:11 and 1QH 6:3-36 (*vid. infra*, p. 22 n.2), the title "Finder of the Community" would be as appropriate for the composer of these hymns as "Founder"!

[3] 22 U, 25 X and 32 F^1, where there is no claim to have founded the Community.

[4] 1 A, 6 F, 19 R, 20 S, 21 T, 23 V, 27 Z and 29 C^1.

Piecing together the references in the Founder hymns to the
author's experiences, one can establish the following outline
of his pilgrimage.

Aware of his own unworthiness before God, he had sought to
serve him amongst his own people (5:23), but they rejected
the revelations he received and were prepared to divulge
the secret which God had sealed in him (5:24f.).[1] This opposition was a source of deep distress to the author (5:6-8,
7:1-5) and led to his exile (4:8f.) and the formation of
the Community (4:24f.). He found vindication, for all the
suffering he had endured, through his position in the Community (2:35-37, 7:6-9). He became in his own person a
criterion, so that transgressors could be distinguished
from the penitent by the way they responded to his work
(2:8-15, 7:12). Later, sickness threatened to hinder his
ministry (8:26-9:7). This outline enables us to establish the
order of the Founder hymns: 10 J, 5 E, 9 I, 2 B, 13 L, 11 J,
8 H, 16 O/17 P. Other hymns, probably by the Founder, are
too fragmentary or too short to be placed in the above
sequence: 3 C, 4 D, 7 G, 12 K. Other short or fragmentary
hymns are more likely to have been composed for, or by
individual members: 14 M, 15 N, 18 Q, 24 W, 26 Y, 28 A^1,
30 D^1 and 31 E^1.

---

[1] Perhaps this secret was a messianic claim. See Black, *loc. cit.*
If the men of 5:23 were the Chasidim who joined the Maccabees (I Macc.
2:42, cf. CD 20:14f.), they may have divulged his secret to the latter.

CHAPTER I: THE SOTERIOLOGY OF THE EMERGING QUMRAN COMMUNITY

A. THE PRE-ESSENIAN[1] LITERATURE

In 1961 Maurice Baillet published a document from Cave 4
(4Q Dib Ham) which G. Vermes has since rendered into English
and entitled, "The Words of the Heavenly Lights".[2] Baillet
dates the manuscript palæographically from the middle of
the second century B.C. and judges it to be pre-Essenian
because of the complete absence of the characteristic
theology of the Community. In certain respects, however,
the document seems to set the tone for the thinking of the
later Community, as we shall see. Most of the fragment is
a prayer for forgiveness on behalf of Israel. At the end
there is another section entitled "Hymns for the Sabbath
Day".

The prayer for forgiveness is a typical piece of post-
exilic piety in the manner of the great doxologies of
judgement in Ezra 9, Neh. 9 and Dan. 9. In it the justice[3]

---

[1] The present writer accepts the identification of the Qumran community
with the Essenes of Philo, Josephus and Pliny the Elder as the most probable hypothesis. The seeming discrepancies can be explained as the natural differences between the inside and the outside view of a movement.

[2] Maurice Baillet, "Un recueil liturgique de Qumrân, grotte 4: 'les
paroles des luminaires'," *Rev. Bib.*, 68 (1961), pp. 195-250; G. Vermes,
The Dead Sea Scrolls in English, London, 1965, pp. 202ff.

[3] The meaning of צדקה (6:3) is extended here to include God's remedial
punishment. In the O.T. this term seems never to bear an unambiguously
punitive sense, but I cannot go as far as G. von Rad in asserting that
this is excluded by definition (*Old Testament Theology*, I, Edinburgh,
p. 377), or in reducing the O.T. concept of righteousness to "faithfulness to the relationship" (*ibid.*, pp. 370ff.), thus dissolving the idea
of conformity to an ethical norm. Throughout the O.T. צדק cognates are
found in forensic contexts, often along with cognates of שפט (Lev. 19:15,
Deut. 16:18, II Sam. 15:4, Isa. 1:21, 11:1, Jer. 11:20, Ezek. 45:9, Pss.
7:11, 9:4, 8, 11:7, 51:4, 82:2, 98:9). It is even asserted that God himself conforms with this norm (Gen. 18:25, Ezek. 18:29). Recent German
scholarship suggests that for Israel God's righteousness had its origin
in his ordering of creation for his creature's well being (P. Stuhlmacher,
Gerechtigkeit Gottes bei Paulus, Göttingen, 1965; H. Graf von Reventlow,
Rechtfertigung im Horizont des Alten Testaments, Munich, 1971; H.H.
Schmidt, "Schöpfung, Gerechtigkeit und Heil, 'Schöpfungstheologie' als
Gesamthorizont biblischer Theologie," *Z. Theo. K.*, 70 (1973), pp. 1-19.

of God's punishment of Israel is acknowledged and its reforming purpose appreciated, whilst Israel casts herself upon the
sheer grace of God as her only hope of salvation. The intention is clearly to fulfil Lev. 26:40-42, in order that God
may graciously bring Israel's exile to a close.[1] It is taken
for granted that the prophecies of a Return had not yet been
fulfilled,[2] and that God was still punishing Israel by afflic-
ting the Holy Land itself.[3] As in Lev. 26, it is not the
remedial punishment itself which is saving, but the acceptance of it as deserved. What is new here, in comparison with
Leviticus, is the insistence that this acceptance is accomplished by God's inward strengthening and by his spirit of
holiness,[4] a theme which is to become prominent in the later
Qumran literature.

God's forgiveness in this document means the end of his
wrath.[5] It is motivated by the very nature of God and by his
faithfulness to his covenant and concern for his reputation.[6]
The author is encouraged to ask God to forgive Israel by the
contemplation of His former kindness to her in the time of

Schmidt traces this idea back to Ancient Near-Eastern creation myths
which purported to explain the origins not only of things, but also of
society and its norms). The connection between God's righteousness and
his salvation follows naturally from this concept, but so does his
punitive justice.

[1] 6:5f. follows closely the language of Lev. 26:41. At the same time it
explains how the author understood the verse: to accept the punishment of
iniquity עוון רצה is to accept God's chastisements, viz. to endure them
rather than revolt against them and break the covenant.

[2] 6:12ff.

[3] 5:3-6. This, together with the reference to God's faithfulness
(5:6-9), forms a further link with Lev. 26 (see verses 31-35).

[4] 5:15; but cf. Deut. 30:6 which mentions the activity of God in connection with this repentance.

[5] In 2:8f. this is linked with Moses' atonement and in 6:2-11 with
Israel's acceptance of the punishment due.

[6] 2:9, 12 and 6:3, 9f., 15.

Moses (2:7-11) and of David (4:5-8). In connection with the
former, Moses' work of atonement is described in the same
language as is used in Exod. 32:30,[1] כיא כפר מושה בעד חטאתם.
Clearly it was believed that Moses had indeed achieved an
atonement for Israel after the worship of the golden calf,
although the Exodus text speaks merely of his intention to
make atonement. After declaring this intention, Moses offered himself in the place of the people, ordered the people to
strip off their ornaments to show their contrition, removed
the tabernacle from the midst of the camp of the guilty and
pleaded with God for the nation.[2] Unfortunately this document does not specify which of these actions achieved the
atonement. The immediate context speaks of God's regard for
his covenant and for his reputation. Now Moses used these
points in his argument with Yahweh in Exod. 32:11-13 and in
33:15. Was his intercession then the means of the atonement?
The question does not seem to have been of consuming interest
to this author. Moses' atonement is merely part of the story
of how God forgave Israel in the past. Far more pertinent to
Israel's present situation were Moses' words in Deut. 28 and
30 and in Lev. 26.[3]

It should be noted that 6:5f., "accepting the punishment of
the iniquities of the fathers", is an importation of the
language of Lev. 26:39 into the citation of verse 41. This
form of the citation is clearly uninfluenced by Ezekiel's
individualism.[4] The cause is probably not ignorance or rejection of Ezekiel's teaching, but a massive emphasis on
Lev. 26 in the thinking of the group which developed this
liturgy.

---

[1]   2:9f. Note that the similarity extends to the preposition which is
used after כפר.

[2]   Exod. 32:31-33:16.

[3]   See end of col. 3.

[4]   Ezek. 18.

Probably from this same period is the apocryphal psalm contained in 11QPs^a[1] (Ps. 154 or Syriac Psalm II[2]). Sanders has
argued that this is pre-Essenian or Chasidic in character.[3]
Certainly it mentions gatherings of the pious in verses 1-4,
12-14. From the point of view of atonement it is interesting
to note that God accepts, יריצה, one who praises him as much
as one who offers many sacrifices (vss. 10f.). Immediately
after this the assemblies of the godly are mentioned, where
there is singing, eating, drinking and meditation on the Law.
The idea is already taking shape that a community with its
religious activities can take the place of the temple and
its sacrifices.

Another fragment which may date from this period is the
Aramaic 4QNab.[4] There is nothing specifically "Essene" in
this document, which is reminiscent of Nebuchadrezzar's doxology in Dan. 4. It tells how Nabonidus was cured from a
tumour by a Jewish exorcist, though he had supplicated his
idols in vain for seven years. This Jew is said to have
"pardoned" his sins. Presumably this means that he effectively assured the king of God's pardon by mediating the cure.
If this is the meaning when a human being is the subject of
a verb of pardoning (where it is the pardon of sins against
God), we may ask what would be the meaning when a human being
is the subject of the verb כפר?[5]

B. HYMNS BY THE FOUNDER OF THE COMMUNITY IN 1QH

In the following pages the longer and less fragmentary hymns
of the Community's founder will be analysed for their soterio-

---

[1] J.A. Sanders, *The Dead Sea Psalms Scroll*, Ithaca, N.Y., 1967, pp. 104-
107.

[2] M. Delcor, *Les Hymnes de Qumran (Hodayot)*, Paris, 1962, pp. 302-312
and appendix.

[3] *Op. cit.*, pp. 104f. and note חסידים, vs. 12.

[4] Vermes, *op. cit.*, p. 229, Dupont-Sommer, *The Essene Writings*, pp. 321-
325.

[5] For כפר with the meaning "forgive" *vid. infra*, pp. 124ff.

logical ideas, one at a time and in the putative chronological order indicated above.[1] An attempt will then be
made to delineate the course of the development of these
ideas. This will provide a framework against which the more
fragmentary Founder hymns will be examined. This part of
the study will then conclude with a summary of the main findings concerning atonement in the context of the soteriology
of these hymns.

C. THE FOUNDER'S TRAVAIL

Hymn 10 J (5:20-39) is filled with almost unrelieved gloom.
The only consolation is that God has not yet forsaken the
author (5:20), for He is on the side of the righteous, the
humble and the oppressed[2] and will deliver from the tumult
together[3] all the poor men of faithfulness (חסד).[4] This
assurance of God's support constitutes a broad space in his

---

[1] *Supra*, pp. 7f.

[2] The syntax of 5:21f. is difficult to sort out due to lacunae in the
text. Translators differ as to precisely who is being delivered and how.
The following interpretation is based on the translation of Vermes (*op.
cit.*, p. 166), since this contains only those soteriological elements
which can be confidently posited in the circumstances.

[3] יחד is here used as an adverb, as in the O.T. In 1QH this usage is
still more frequent (4:24, 5:22f., 30, 6:13, 8:5, 10:34, 11:25f) than
the meaning "Community" (3:22, 23, 11:14 and 14:18). All the adverbial
uses except the last two occur in material by the Founder, but the meaning "Community" never occurs in this material. These passages cast some
light on the genesis of the term "Community". It expresses the Group's
oneness with the angels and with all creatures subject to God (3:21-23,
11:11-14). The members are in the same council (סוד, 11:12, 14:18) with
the holy ones. Their lot (3:22, 11:11) is with the spirits (3:22, 11:12)
of knowledge and understanding (3.23, 11.13, 14:19) for eternity (3:30ff.,
11:13). In 6:13, where the term is used adverbially by the Founder, a
similar theme is expressed.

For the view that יחד is already a noun in the O.T., see S. Talmon,
"The Sectarian יחד," *Vetus Testamentum*, 3 (1953), pp. 133-140. For a
derivation of the Qumran term יחד from the Greek concept τὸ κοινόν, see
Dombrowski, "היחד in 1QS and τὸ κοινόν," *Harvard Theological Review*,
59 (1966), pp. 293-307.

[4] Perhaps this is a reference to the Chasidim, or at least to those
amongst them who were worthy of the name.

heart in spite of the straits into which his enemies had
brought him (5:32f.). Clearly these are triumphing over
him. They even sing taunt songs and there is no standing
before them (5:29f.). These enemies are termed his com-
panions, those who entered into his covenant and those who
were joined to his council, but it does not follow that they
were members of the Qumran community.[1] Rather, this conflict
was the birth travail out of which the Community was to emerge
later.[2] So great is the author's distress expressed in this
hymn, that he is unlikely to be merely talking about the de-
fection of members from a community of which he was the acknowledged head and of which he was later revered as the
founder. A more likely hypothesis is that the hymn reflects
a violent power struggle resulting in the defeat and exile of
the author. The activity of his enemies constitutes the only
Unheil[3] in this hymn. Though the main cause of the author's
distress is the effect of this opposition on himself, he does
intimate that it also threatened to hinder God's work, for
they have betrayed and vilified the secret which God revealed
in him (5:25) and they alter the deeds of God in their guilt
(5:36). Nevertheless, because of their sin, God hid the
counsel of his truth from them (5:24f.). The text of the
hymn closes with fragments which seem to refer to an eternal
imprisonment, but it is difficult to see whether this threat-
ens the poet or his enemies.

Hymn 5 E (3:5-18) takes up the imagery of 10 J: the birth
pangs (3:7-10, cf. 5:30f.) and the everlasting imprisonment

---

[1] When the community is formed, it is not referred to as the men of "my
covenant" or "my council" (though 14:18, סוד, may be an exception, *vid.
infra*, pp. 42f.), but as God's covenant (4:24, 10:27-31, 18:24, 28) and
the council of the truth and the holy ones (2:10, 4:24f., 5:9).

[2] Cf. 5:30f. and 3:7-10. *Vid infra*, pp. 15f.

[3] This German word designates the opposite of salvation (*Heil*). "Un-
saved condition" is sometimes awkward in English and lacks the general
significance of <u>anything</u> from which a man might seek deliverance by divine
power. The very posture of praise, present in all these hymns, implies
that God has done for the worshipper something that he could not do for
himself. This is salvation in the broadest sense, and it implies salvation <u>from</u> something.

(3:16-18, cf. 5:36f.). The former is greatly extended
through the author's expectation of what is to be brought
forth by means of his travail and through a generalization
of the image to include the final tribulation which is to
come upon the whole world, leading to the birth of the viper[1]
and culminating in the everlasting imprisonment of evil and
the spirit that produces it (3:18).[2] The birth pangs of the
author are already intense, but the birth has not yet taken
place.[3] The birth pangs of evil have not yet reached their
full intensity,[4] but it seems to be implied that they are
hastened on by the imminence of the birth of the "wonderful
counsellor" mentioned in 3:10. This line takes up the
messianic prophecy of Isa. 9:6 and applies it to the birth
of the Community. For Qumran, the wonderful counsellor is
one to whom has been revealed God's wonderful counsel.[5]
He knows what God is about to do, for, like the prophets, he
has heard God planning it.[6] Salvation in this hymn is both
for the Founder and for the members of the Community which
is about to be born. At such a time both mother (3:9) and
child (3:8) are threatened by death. Deliverance in such

---

[1] The viper is probably iniquity and its mother the spirit of iniquity.

[2] The kind of ultimate destiny envisaged at Qumran for the powers of
evil and their human agents can be determined only after the study of
several passages. Clearly the present section reflects the kind of thinking exemplified in I Enoch 10-12, 21, 27, 108.

[3] See the tenses used in 3:7-10.

[4] See the tenses used in 3:10-13.

[5] פלא, "wonderful", is rather a rare word in the O.T. It is much more
frequent in the Scrolls, probably because of this identification of the
Community with the "wonderful counsellor" of Isaiah. עצה "counsel",
should be so translated in the earlier Qumran literature whenever possible, rather than as "council", which suggests men being consulted.
Here, they are rather informed of what God has already decided to do,
and this is high honour indeed. For an evaluation of God's council in
the O.T. see Th. C. Vriezen, *The Religion of Ancient Israel*, London,
1967, p. 36.

By 1QSa 1:26f., 2:2, עצה had come to mean "council".

[6] Cf. I Kings 22:19-23, Amos 3:7.

a situation is presumably to be sought in the saving power
of God. Unfortunately the early lines of the composition have
been severely damaged, but Mansoor and others find the word
ותצילני "and thou hast delivered me" in line 5. Certainly,
if this is the correct reading, it must be interpreted as a
reference to his confidence in a concrete expression of God's
deliverance soon to be manifested, since the tense patterns
in the rest of the hymn suggest that he is still in the pain
of travail and has not yet safely brought the Community to
birth.

Dupont-Sommer[1] detects a redeeming work for the Messiah and
his mother in 3:9f., which he translates: "and in the bonds
of Sheol there shall spring from the crucible of the Pregnant One a marvellous counsellor with his might: and he shall
deliver every man from the billows because of Her who is big
with him." עם גברתו ויפלט   ובחבלי שאול יגיח מכור הריה פלא יועץ
גבר ממשברים בהריתו. This translation depends on pointing ויפלט
as a pi'el, translating גבר as "every man" and משברים as
"breakers of the sea" instead of as "birth pains". The pointing of יפלט will have to depend on what the context demands.
If it is a qal, it means "that he may escape", or something
of the kind. There is, however, only one instance of the qal
in the Old Testament. גבר appears to continue the reference
to Isa. 9:6, where the cognate גבור occurs.[2] It would more
naturally refer to the wonderful counsellor than to every man.
The word does not mean a human being as such, but a male child
or a male of military age. Dupont-Sommer's translation suggests salvation through the Messiah-child and his mother for
every man, but the word means *vir*, not *homo*. Though the plu-
ral משברים means "breakers of the sea" in the Old Testament,
the singular being used for "birth pains" or "matrix", the
latter sense is more appropriate in the present context, since
the sea-faring imagery does not re-appear until line 12. Although, therefore, some *prima facie* probability attaches to

---

[1] *The Essene Writings*, p. 208.

[2] The word has already been alluded to by the phrase עם גבורתו "with his
might", earlier in line 10.

Dupont-Sommer's renderings of ויפלט and משברים because of the
usual Old Testament meanings of these forms, in the present
context these renderings have necessitated a forced interpretation of גבר and have introduced soteriological ideas not
attested elsewhere in the Scrolls.[1] Furthermore, משברים occurs again in line 11, where Dupont-Sommer's translation ac-
knowledges that it bears the meaning "matrix". It is unlikely that the same word would have a different meaning in the
previous line. It is also rather forced to read a saving
significance into the preposition in בהריתו. The local sense
fits the context better and the passage may be translated:
"and in the throes of hell there shall break forth from the
crucible of her that is pregnant a wonderful counsellor with
his might, so that a mighty one shall escape from the pains
of childbirth in her that is pregnant with him."

D.   THE FOUNDER AND THE COMMUNITY

   In the hymns considered so far the author had received no
concrete token of God's salvation. Massive unfaithfulness to
God had taken place in the group to which he belonged, but
the new group had not yet been formed. In contrast, hymn 9 I
(5:5-19) exhales an atmosphere of profound relief. At the
same time there is a sense of sin displayed in this hymn
which was not evident in the hymns we have attributed to the
earlier period of intense conflict with his enemies. It is
no longer simply a matter of his own innocence and his op-
ponents' sinfulness. The oppressors amongst whom he sojourned
are seen as God's instruments of judgement for the punishment
of the wicked and even for the chastisement of the author
(5:6-9).

   Salvation in this hymn is for the author himself, styled
God's afflicted (עני 5:13, 14) and His poor one (אביון 5:16).
He has been saved from the judgement which he deserved for
his own sin (5:5f.). What this judgement would have been is
intimated by the thrice repeated phrase, "thou hast not for-

---

[1]   The closest would be the possible implication of a saving work for the
Messiah in CD 14:18f. *Vid. infra*, pp. 96f.

saken me . . ." (עזבתני לא 5:5, 6, 12). This is already the
experience of Ps. 22:24 and the opposite of the opening verses
of that Psalm (למה עזבתני). God's abandonment had threatened
to leave him in the power of dire internal and external foes.
The internal foe was his own sinful inclination (5:6), the
external foe, his enemies, whom he likens to fishers seeking
his life (5:7f.) and to lions longing to tear the prey (passim)[.]
In all this there was a threat not only to his physical life,
but also to his relationship with God (5:6). The latter aspect he will elaborate in later hymns.[2] Salvation came to
the author by chastisement through patience. The very trials
through which he was saved constituted one of the means of his
salvation. He was placed among the lions for judgement (5:8f.)
and this judgement had a salvific effect upon him, for thereby
his determination to do the will of God was strengthened (5:9,
11). He had been purified like gold seven times in the fur-
nace.[3] In his distress he had cried out to God (5:12) and
God had heard him, though it seems that he had to wait for a
concrete demonstration of God's salvation. During the waiting time he was preserved from physical destruction and the
Law was safe within his heart. Thus the spiritual lessons
he was learning would not be lost and would one day benefit
others too (5:8-15). The result of all this is ultimately
that there is a great calm in his own soul (5:18), and also
that he becomes an example of God's might before men and the
bearer of an insight into the mind of God which can serve as
the basis of a covenant for all who seek it (5:9).

---

[1]   Hab. 1:6-17 seems to form part of the background to this theme. There
the Chaldeans are likened to leopards and other wild animals and their
activity is described in terms of catching fish. Yet they are ordained
to be executors of God's judgement. Cf. Hos. 5:8-6:6.

[2]   *Vid. infra*, pp. 20f., 26, 29f.

[3]   This may be an allusion to the kind of thinking elaborated in Lev. 26,
where Israel is repeatedly threatened with a seven-fold punishment for her
sins. The punishment includes exile (cf. 1QH 5:5) and results in an acceptance of God's punishment as just and a return to the covenant (Lev.
26:42 and 44, cf. 1QH 5:9). The "seven times" does not mean that the
sinner had received more punishment than he deserved, but only that previous remedial punishment, which had not yet proven effective, was multi-
plied. In point of fact the punishment was less than deserved (1QH 5:5f.).

In hymn 2 B (2:5-19) the Community begins to come into focus. Salvation is not only for the author, but through him
for those who follow his teaching. Already his earlier
frightening experiences have receded far enough into the
background for him to be able to take a very confident attitude toward his enemies and to see his own role in a more
detached way as a criterion by which God judges between the
faithful and the wicked. This does not cause him to lose his
emerging sense of sin. He knows that his lips are unworthy
for the task God has committed to him (2:7). This work seems
to be to instruct a group which is forming and it is the
formation of this group which gives him an attitude of confidence in the face of opposition. The performance of this
task constitutes his answer to his enemies' insults (2:7-9).

Salvation from the taunts of the wicked comes for the Founder, then, through the formation of the Community, but he is
able to bring this about only by the endurance which God himself has given him (2:7f.). Besides this, the author has become in his own person a means of salvation for his disciples
and at the same time a means of damnation for the wicked.
He condemns the unrighteous by becoming an occasion for sin
in them (2:10) through arousing their opposition (2:16).[1]
Doubtless they are jealous of his leadership in the newly-
formed group. Thus the very thing, which brings salvation
to the faithful (2:8f., 10, 13), brings damnation to the
wicked: his successful teaching activity in the Community.
The disciples are saved through the truth which the Founder
teaches, but also through the trial to which he subjects them
(2:13f.). It is not yet clear whether this "trial" refers
already to the beginnings of the Community discipline later
elaborated in 1QS and CD, or simply indicates that even the
disciples would have to make a hard decision to follow the
Founder, in view of the controversy which he had aroused outside of the group.

The theme of the Founder as a criterion between the right-

---

[1] Dupont-Sommer and Delcor's translations.

eous and the wicked is continued in hymn 13 L (7:6-25),
but the underlying theme is now the divine support. It is
more greatly stressed than before that he owes everything to
the grace of God.[1] The hymn also develops the theme of the
covenant which had been mentioned in 9 I and thereby helps
to clarify the statement in that hymn that out of the counsel
of truth which God had fortified in his heart there would
issue a covenant for those who seek it (5:9). Hymn 13 L
stresses that the author has been faithful and dedicated to
the covenant and that this attitude is a gift from God himself (7:8, 10, 19f.). This is equivalent to the statement
in 5:9 that God had fortified a counsel of truth in his heart.
God's counsel is all that is in His mind.[2] It is not only
what He plans to do, but also what He wills man to do. It
is Law as well as prophecy, for it is the decree of the King.
Now the Law is the content of the Covenant as regards the ob-
ligations which man undertakes towards God. During his trials
the Founder had been tempted to abandon the covenant, but God
had strengthened his spirit and prevented this fall from
grace (7:8).

The author feels himself to have been saved from his enemies
and from his own sin, whether actual (7:17) or potential (7:9).
This salvation has been effected by the power and goodness of
God alone (7:6-10, 16-19), which has taken effect through the
revelation of the truth from God as to what man's conduct
should be (7:13-15, 20). The determination to follow the path
thus prescribed is attributed to the spirit of holiness which
God has instilled into him (7:6f.). His salvation results in

---

[1] 7:16-18 contains several lacunæ, but there is general agreement on the
sense of the section as a whole. The hymnist seems to be saying there
that he can be saved from sin neither through wealth, nor through power,
nor even through his own righteous works, but through God's goodness
alone.

[2] סוד, see Mansoor, *The Thanksgiving Hymns*, p. 105, n. 16. Ps. 25:14,
referred to in that note, throws considerable light on 1QH 5:9 too, for
it places the covenant in parallel with the סוד as the content of God's
revelation to the faithful. In 1QH 7:10 the term עצה is introduced and
brought into connection with the covenant concept. עצה is a characteristically Qumran word as a near synonym for סוד.

a tremendous sense of security (7:8f.) and everlasting
glory, light[1] and peace (7:14f., 24f.). It is difficult
to say whether an after-life or resurrection doctrine is
implied here, but it is clear that the author sees an eternal
significance in his work. This is because it is to have a
messianic issue. The wonderful counsellor whose birth was
spoken of in Isa. 9 is to reign for ever (Isa. 9:7). This
same counsellor is called in Isa. 11:1 "a branch" (נצר).
1QH 7:19 uses the same term to designate what the Founder is
about to produce.[2] He also refers to his disciples by the
same term as is used for the associates of Joshua the high
priest, the men to whom the Messiah was to appear.[3] The
author's salvation, then, is not for himself only. It includes the service he has to perform in the group (7:20-22).
Once more there is a double soteriological reference. Salvation is for the Founder, but it is also for the Community
members whom he terms the sons of חסד and the "men of wonder"[4]
(7:20f.). For these the way of salvation is to imbibe the
Founder's teachings like an infant at its mother's breast
(7:20-22).

---

[1] "and I shall shine in a seven-fold light . . . for thy glory", (7:24;
Vermes, *op. cit.*, p. 174). Isa. 30:26 and 60:19-22 obviously form part
of the background to the thought here (*vid.* Delcor, *op. cit.*, p. 194f.,
n. and Mansoor, *The Thanksgiving Hymns*, p. 151, n. 4). It is also possible that the author thinks of himself in terms of the seven-branched
candlestick in the temple, for this sacred object figures in Zech. 4 and
there are probably already two references to Zech. 3 in this hymn: the
expression "men of wonder" (*ibid.*, n. 2) and the reference to the "branch"
in line 19 (cf. Zech. 3:8, though there the word is צמח, not נצר as in
1QH 7:19).

[2] Furthermore the idea of counsel is again applied to the coming one in
Isa. 11:2: עצה. This becomes a favourite term in the Qumran literature
and is already used in 1QH 7:10 in connection with the emerging Community.

[3] Mansoor, *loc. cit.* Zech. 3:8.

[4] J.T. Milik (*Ten Years of Discovery in the Wilderness of Judaea*, Naperville, Illinois, 1958, p. 77) suggests that this may refer to the Chasidim.
See also *supra*, p. 13 n. 4.

The beginning of hymn 11 J (6:3-36) is badly damaged. It
includes terms which may relate to the danger from which the
author has been delivered: scorn, ruin and destruction (6:2f.).
The nature of the author's *Unheil* is further indicated in the
phrase, "the assembly of violence" (6:5). This group was
probably identical either with the men who are said in line
19 to have been led astray from the author's testimony, or
with those who led them astray. He likened the ordeal through
which he had passed to a storm at sea and the salvation into
which God had brought him to a fortified city (6:22-29). This
city is the Community, founded on the truth (6:25). It functions as a means of salvation for the author. There he has
found those who reprove justly and God has opened his ear to
their discipline (6:4).[1] There no stranger or enemy would be
allowed to penetrate (6:27f.). The exclusive character of the
Community was an indispensible element in its ability to save.
Here it is no longer the Community which finds salvation through
the author, but the author who finds it through the Community.[2]
During the time of his ordeal he had found comfort in the
knowledge that there is hope for those who repent (6:6f.).
Undoubtedly he felt himself to be one of these repentant ones
and was sustained by this hope during his trials. He is conscious that God has taken him into his counsel (עצה) along
with the angels of the Presence (6:5, 12f.).

---

[1] Following Delcor's reconstruction (*op. cit.*, p. 172). Unfortunately
most of the letters are either missing or very obscure, except for the
words, "thou hast opened my ears . . . those who reprove in justice."

[2] This does not mean that the author was not the Founder, but only that
the term "Founder" may be somewhat of a misnomer. The description of the
ordeal through which he had passed (6:19-24) clearly identifies him with
the author of the other hymns we have ascribed to the "Founder". Although
the author did not actually found the Community, he thoroughly informed
it with his own ideas and ideals.

According to CD 1:8-12, the Community was in existence for twenty years
before the Teacher of Righteousness started his ministry in its midst.
During this time they seem to have had a sense of guilt, but no sense of
salvation.

A parallel situation existed in modern history. Adolf Hitler did not
found the party which he later led. He discovered it already in existence
in 1919. Nevertheless, he functioned virtually as the founder, since the
party was indelibly marked with the imprint of his personality and ambi-
tions.

This hymn is notable for its vision of the Community's
future mission and its place in God's saving activity. It
is to be a remnant purified from guilt (6:7f.). This purification is to be effected by obedience on the part of the
Community members and by God's kindness in justifying them
(6:8f.), and it will consist in God's instructing them according to his truth, leading them to obey his law (6:9f.,
14). God has done this for his own glory and as a result his
mighty deeds will be contemplated by all nations for evermore
(6:10-12).[1] The members of the Community are to share the
lot of the angels of the Presence (6:13). The following
sentence seems to state that in consequence they need no
angelic intercessor or mediator, but a hole in the MS makes
the text obscure (6:13f.). The eternal and universal extent
of the Community's influence is first described in terms of
the growth of a plant (6:15-17); then the image is suddenly
changed to that of an eternal light, but it is a burning
light in whose flames the guilty will be destroyed (6:18f.).
Later the author pictures the Community as a fortified city
in which the godly will be kept safe until the time comes for
the destruction of all the ungodly at the hands of the sons
of truth (6:24-33).[2] Line 34 speaks of this resurgence of
the Community's fortunes in terms of a resurrection. There
seems to be an echo of Isa. 26:19, 41:14, Ezek. 37 and Dan.
12:2. If the language were clearly an allusion to the last
of these, there would be no doubt that the author was envis-
aging a literal resurrection here, for that is the unmistak-

---

[1] According to the reconstruction of Dupont-Sommer (*The Essene Writings*,
p. 219) and Delcor (*op. cit.*, p. 176), the end of line 12 states that all
nations have been admitted to God's covenant along with the members of the
Community. Such universalism would have to be well attested elsewhere before it could be accepted as one of the Community's ideas. See the refut-
ation by J. Carmignac: "Les citations de l'Ancien Testament, et spécialement des Poèmes du Serviteur, dans les *Hymnes* de Qumrân," *Rev. Qum.*, 2
(1959/60), pp. 385f.

[2] The eternal gates which are to be opened to allow the weapons of war to
be mobilized in this final conflict are perhaps the doors of the Community
itself. The similarity with the language of Ps. 24:7 may suggest that
they are the gates of heaven (so Delcor, *op. cit.*, p. 183), but the two
thoughts might well be merged in the poetic expression of a group which
felt itself to be united in counsel with the angels of the Presence.

able meaning of the Daniel passage. There is no clear allusion, however, merely echoes, and the passage cannot be pressed to say more than that the faithful remnant, long counted as
a mere worm, has already raised its banner and will triumph
with God's help in the last days.

Most of hymn 8 H (4:5-5:4) appears on a well preserved column of the scroll. Unfortunately, the end of the column, the
only place where there is appreciable damage, is the very
place where atonement ideas are most in evidence. The hymn
breathes something of the sweet odour of confidence and suc-
cess (4:27-29), but the memory of the author's ordeal is still
with him. He has had time to reflect upon the internal as
well as upon the external aspects of his difficult pilgrimage,
so that the sense of sin, already present in 9 I and 13 L, becomes more precise. 9 I referred vaguely to the hymnist's
sinful inclination during his time of trial (5:6). 13 L tells
us that at that time he had been tempted to abandon the covenant (7:8). 8 H elaborates upon the mental process which
threatened to lead in that direction: "I had said in my transgression, 'I have been abandoned by thy covenant.'"[1] The
roots of unfaithfulness lie in unbelief. He had been preserved from the former only by the grace of God (7:5-8). The
latter remained a sin to be confessed, for he had committed
it. His conscience has now become so sensitive that the memory of this sin of doubt causes him emotional distress and a
feeling of extreme physical weakness (4:33f.). His confession
of this sin is linked with a confession of the sins of his
fathers, in the manner of the great post-exilic confessions
of Ezra and Daniel, but this does not constitute a retreat
from a sense of individual responsibility (4:34f.).[2] He has
been delivered from his own guilt (4:33-37) and also from the
schemes of his enemies (4:10). Ultimately he is to be delivered from the latter through their destruction (4:18-23).

---

[1]   4:35. Mansoor (*The Thanksgiving Hymns*, p. 130, n. 8) has pointed out
that the syntax here closely follows the construction of Ps. 31:22 (23
Heb.).

[2]   *Vid. supra*, p. 11.

Though this is to be primarily the work of God himself (4:18-21), the author expects to participate in it with his own hands (4:22). He also states that their punishment is to take the form of their being trapped in their own snares (4:19). This does not mean that their punishment is automatic, but merely that the same thing which they schemed against the author will in the end be inflicted upon them by him.[1] Punishment in these hymns is not the boomerang effect of the sin, but an additional act of God in judgement.[2] God himself never acts falsely. These men have acted falsely and must be destroyed. Only those who act as God acts will be established for ever (4:7f., 20-22).

While awaiting the final destruction of his foes, the author leans upon the One through whose might he is finally to defeat them (4:22) and is strengthened through this trust (4:22, 36, 39). He refers to this interim salvation also as an illumination. It is as welcome as the dawn (4:6), as revealing too. It reveals God's covenant (4:5) and his power in action (4:23). This forms the basis of the author's teaching activity in the community (ibid.). His deliverance from the internal threat, his own guilt, comes also from leaning. He trusts in God's compassion (4:36f.) and this confidence is re-inforced by the memory of God's former kindnesses and His power (4:35f.) as well as by a consideration of the general principles of God's saving ways with man (4:37f.). Since man is sinful from the cradle to the grave and is incapable of attaining righteousness and perfection by his own effort (4:29-31), he can be saved only by a spirit from God working within him to change his conduct (4:31f.). God does this for the elect (4:32f.). It is God who has created both the righteous and the wicked (4:38). 15:13-22 develops this sentiment in the direction of an uncompromising statement of double predestination, but this doctrine is probably indicated here too.[3]

---

[1] See Delcor, op. cit., p. 143.

[2] See Becker, op. cit., p. 59.

[3] Cf. ibid: "bei diesen Psalmen . . . prädestinatianische Gedanken völlig fehlen."

God's compassion, on which the poet leans for his salvation, is manifested in the divine forgiveness. The construction with כפר used in 4:37 (with no preposition to denote the sin atoned for) is not very frequent in the Old Testament. With עוון as here, it occurs only in Dan. 9:24 and Ps. 78:38. The latter is more likely to be the background of the present passage. The theme of Ps. 78 is God's compassionate forgive- ness of Israel when she had been untrue to the covenant. This is stated to involve the putting away of the divine wrath by God himself in his awareness of human frailty (Ps. 78:37-39). The same themes are present in this hymn: God's compassion (4:35-37), sin against the covenant (4:35, cf. 7:8), the sin- fulness and frailty of human nature (4:29f.). The theme of God's wrath is also present (4:18-21), and the choice of the term כפר עוון to express forgiveness here is most naturally accounted for on the assumption that the author wishes to express the fact that in pardoning God puts away his wrath. This He does in his צדקה, the characteristic term for God's saving righteousness (4:37). The purpose of God's grace to- wards the unworthy is that they may know all his righteous works. If none were pardoned and enabled to live righteously, mankind would not know God's righteous works and his power and goodness in having them performed in spite of human frailty and sin (4:30-33).

As usual, the author has something to say about the salva- tion of his disciples. Not for them the destruction decreed upon the men of falsehood, for they walk in the way of God's heart and he takes pleasure in them (4:20-24, 32f.). There is little doubt that they have learned the way of God's heart from the author himself. They have had no cause to regret this (4:23f.). The illumination which the author had received (4:5, 23) was now upon the faces of his followers (4:27). They will stand before God for ever (4:21f.) and their cause will always triumph (4:25).[1] They will enter the council of

---

[1] If the latter statement is taken as explanatory of the former, there is not necessarily any eternal life doctrine in lines 21f.

the angels and have direct access to God himself (4:24f.).[1]
In the last days they will be instruments of God's vengeance
upon all who transgress his commandments, whether Jew or Gentile (4:26f.).

E. THE FOUNDER'S SICKNESS

Both the end of column 8 and the beginning of 9 describe a
severe illness. It is a disease involving fever (8:30),
debility (8:32), depression and sleeplessness (8:29f., 9:4f.).
It is very likely that both columns belong to the same hymn
(16 O/17 P), which would thus be the longest in the scroll.[2]
The extreme physical weakness, which in 8 H is attributed
to a bad conscience, is by now clearly seen to be due to disease. Apparently he felt that his disease was caused by an
enemy's accusation before the heavenly tribunal (9:3, 8f.).[3]
The hymn is in three main sections:-
(a) the allegory of the plantation by the watercourse, with
     the author as the irrigator (8:4-26);
(b) the sickness by which this work has been hindered (8:26-
     9:9);
(c) the author's acceptance of this judgement upon him and
     his confidence in God's love (9:9-36).
Though the sections are dissimilar in content, they are connected in a way which is indicated above by the words under-
lined.

The hymn opens with a declaration that the author has been
placed near a fountain of living water in the midst of the
trees of life. The roots of these trees are to grow down
into the watercourse itself and then sprout a branch (נצר

---

[1] Following Mansoor's hint that Ps. 5:3 (4 Heb.) provides a clue to the
meaning here (*The Thanksgiving Hymns*, p. 127 n. 8).

[2] So M. Wallenstein, *The Nezer and the Submission in Suffering Hymn from
the Dead Sea Scrolls*, Istanbul, 1957, and Vermes, *op. cit.*, pp. 176-182.
Even if, with Dupont-Sommer and Delcor, we understand 8:35f. as saying
that in spite of his sickness, he is not to be silenced, the hymn is
still to be judged a unity, since a similar sentiment is expressed in
9:8f.

[3] Cf. S. Mowinkel's interpretation of certain Psalms (e.g. Ps. 6): *The
Psalms in Israel's Worship*, II, Oxford, 1962, pp. 2-4, 6-8. The foes can
be either human or supernatural.

8:4-7). This branch will become an eternal fountain,[1] but it
will function as such only for those who believe in it (8:8,
13f.). For unbelievers, called here birds and beasts, it is
just a tree with leaves to be used or abused at their convenience (8:8f.). Some of the unbelievers are termed "the
trees by the water" (8:6, 9 עצי מים), a phrase probably culled
from Ezek. 31:14, where it refers to the great ones of the
earth who despise the people of God. These "trees by the
water" will flourish at first, though their roots do not extend into the watercourse itself, whilst the trees from which
the נצר is sprouting will be ignored (8:9-11).[2] The exclusion
of unbelievers is not only the natural consequence of their
ignoring the Branch and the trees of life which have caused it
to sprout, it is also an additional and deliberate act of God
in judgement, expressed here in terms of the angels with fiery
swords preventing sinful man from reaching the fruit of the
tree of life (8:11-14). This fruit is the same thing as the
water which is available from the Branch-turned-fountain. It
seems that the watercourse is the teaching of the Law,[3] that

---

[1] The imagery, of course, is quite grotesque, but the hymnist is talking
not about real trees and water supplies, but about the Community and the
teaching of the Law. For similar imagery cf. Zech. 4:12.

[2] למטעה אמת . . . ומפריח נצר in line 10 clearly echoes להפריח נצר למטעה
עולם in line 6. The subject of the verb in line 6 is clearly the trees,
representing the Community. The Community is likely to be the subject
also in line 10, although grammatically the subject cannot be the trees
since the participle is singular. Dupont-Sommer thinks the Teacher of
Righteous caused the sprouting in line 10 (*The Essene Writings*, p. 227,
n. 1), whilst Delcor thinks the subject is God (*op. cit.* p. 203).

[3] Cf. Ps. Sol. 14:1-4, CD 3:16, 6:4. According to Dupont-Sommer (*The
Essene Writings*, p. 225, n. 2) the watercourse is the Teacher of Righteousness himself. His translation seems to be based on the reading כמקור
in line 4, not במקור. Although this scribe writes כ very much like ב,
there does seem to be a discernible difference in the way he writes the
two letters. He tends to make a corner in כ at the top right and in ב at
the bottom right. According to this criterion it is clearly ב here (see
The Dead Sea Scrolls of the Hebrew University, ed. E.L. Sukenik, Jerusalem, 1955, plate 42). Furthermore, a כ here does not make such good
sense, since it would mean that the watercourse symbolized the author in
line 4, but his teaching in line 7 (where it is unlikely that the poet is
calling himself the "fountain of life") and in line 16 (where the spring
is not identical with the author, but is said to be in his mouth), and
that the Teacher of Righteousness was both water and irrigator (8:21-26).
Already in 2 B the Founder appears as an irrigator (2:18), where parallel
sentiments in 2:8f., 10 and 13 point to the spring's identity with the Law.

the trees by the water as well as the beasts and the birds
are the powerful men of the earth and the apostate in Israel,
that the "dry ground" alludes to Isaianic passages where the
physical and spiritual exile of Israel is the theme, that the
trees of life are the Community and that the Branch is the
Community in its messianic aspect, which is the same thing
as the restored Israel in the post-exilic eschaton.[1] In lines
15-20 the author changes his images in rapid succession.[2] His
enemies are likened to rivers in spate throwing up mud, the
teaching of the Law to rain in his mouth, then again to a
spring which in turn becomes a destructive torrent, and then
a fire against his enemies, the beasts and the "trees by the
water".[3] This destruction makes room for the Branch to grow
into an Eden of glory.

The hymnist goes on to describe his work in the Community
in terms of that of a skilled irrigator and husbandman (8:21-
24). If he were to stop this work disaster would follow (8:24-
26). He then describes his sickness. The implication in this
context would be that the disease hindered his work. This is
stated explicitly in certain reconstructions of lines 35-37
(Mansoor, Vermes, Wallenstein). He seems to believe that the
proximate cause of this sickness is the malicious accusation
of him by an enemy before God. He is content to leave his
judgement in the hands of God. If God condemns him to receive
stripes, he will gladly accept them, for, like David, he can
discern behind the chastisement the love of the Father for his

---

[1] The return after the edict of Cyrus had not been the promised restoration of Israel. They were still slaves in their own land (Neh. 9:36).
Vid. supra, p. 10.

The immediate Old Testament background of this section is Isa. 60.
Isa. 60:13 is quoted almost verbatim in line 5. The use of נצר here,
which is not a frequent word in the O.T., probably reflects Isa. 60:21.
Allusion to Isa. 11:1 is not entirely absent, for the promises of early
Isaiah about a scion of the house of David who is to reign in eternal
peace and justice are applied in the later chapters of Isaiah to Israel
restored to the land. In Isa. 60:21 the people of Israel is the נצר.

[2] This, together with the many lacunae here, makes the meaning rather uncertain. What is offered in the following two sentences is quite tentative.

[3] For the destructive power of the prophetic word, cf. Jer. 1:10.

son.[1] This gives him confidence to answer all the calumnies
of his foes, for God is not only his judge, but also his ad-
vocate (9:7-9, 20-23). The grounds for this confidence in
God's compassion are God's dealings with him at the time of
his previous trial: God had set a supplication in his mouth,
preserved him physically, kept hope alive within him, imbued
him with the desire to do what is right and forgiven his sin
at that time (9:10-13).[2] His hope is in God's power and goodness, not in his own righteousness. A man may be righteous
or powerful before his fellows, but not before God (9:14-16).
The chastisement he has just received is evidence that God is
on his side. Consequently he has been able to rejoice in this
adversity and even in the scorn of his foes,[3] and is to inherit eternal glory, power, light, liberty and security (9:24-
29). His confidence in God's power and goodness is based both
on God's dealings with him during his former tribulation, and
on an experience of God's fatherly treatment since his birth.
Within his heart God had taught him the truth and sustained
him in a proper attitude by His spirit of holiness, whilst ex-
ternally He had preserved his physical life and chastised him
in justice whenever he sinned (9:29-36). Though this involves
a kind of predestination (9:29f.), it can also be viewed as an
instance of God's universal love for all his creatures (9:36).

---

[1] 9:10, 35f. Cf. II Sam. 7:14. Once again the messianic promise is extended to all the faithful remnant.

[2] This interpretation follows Delcor and Dupont-Sommer in translating the
verb here by the past tense. Mansoor renders it as a future, also Svend
Holm-Nielsen, *Hodayot, Psalms from Qumran*, Aarus, 1960, p. 145. Probably
the "former transgression" was the sin of doubt during his earlier trials
(*vid. supra*, p. 24). It is unlikely to be "the original sin". Attention
was directed towards the glory rather than the sin of Adam at this time
and speculation on the entry of sin into the world seemed to centre on
the giants of Gen. 6:1-4. See I Enoch. 10:8.

[3] It is in this sense that his wounds were turned into healing (9:25),
viz. healing for himself. Black (*The Dead Sea Scrolls and Christian Doctrine*, p. 15) argues from the similarity with 1QH 2:8 that the meaning
here is that the wounds have turned into healing for others. The immediate context does not support this interpretation. In 4Q Dib Ham 2:14f.,
"healing" means a "change of heart". Similarly, in this hymn, the healing is a consequence of his remedial punishment ("wounds").

The hymn elaborates very clearly the idea of accepting God's
punishment (9:9f., 24-26). This is later to become a feature
of Qumran's way of salvation.[1] Here it is not so much a means
of salvation as one of its fruits.

F. ANALYSIS OF THE MAJOR FOUNDER HYMNS

   The following tables set out the salvation ideas of the
hymns probably composed by the Community's founder. The first
table lists from what, to what and through what the author
felt himself to be saved. The second table lists the same
things with respect to Community members. The figures in the
body of the tables indicate the line numbers in the column
concerned where the particular soteriological elements occur.
Those elements which are clearly present in the text but do
not clearly possess the soteriological significance indicated
in the table are enclosed in parentheses. Uncertainty of the
reading or of the translation (e.g. due to lacunæ) is indicated by a question mark before the item concerned.

TABLE I

The author is saved

	from (unheil)	*to*	*through*
10 J 5:20-39 *supra*, 13f.	enemies 23ff. possibility of being forsaken by God 20	interior freedom	God's power 20. Salva- tion is still very much in the future. His hope is based upon God's characteristic help of the poor 21f.
5 E 3:5-18 *supra*, 14-17	tribulation birth pangs 9	produce the wonderful counsellor 9f.	? God's saving power 5 his own tribulation - implication of birth pang imagery 7ff.

---

[1]   E.g. *infra*, pp. 65f, 70, 77ff., 83.

TABLE I cont.

The author is saved

	from	to	through
9 I 5:5-19 *supra*, 17f.	possibility of God's forsaking him in judgement 5f., 12 to his enemies 6-9 and to his own sinful inclination 6 - as he deserved 5	interior calm 18 being an example of God's might 9, 15 being a teacher of others 9 - because he had <u>learned</u> something: the mind of God	being chastised seven times - through his enemies 15f. God's answering his cry of distress 12 God's preserving him physically 13-15, spiritually 6
2 B 2:5-19 *supra*, 19	enemies' taunts 7-9 (? unworthiness of his lips 7)	(endurance in service 7f.) (being a criterion 8-19)	his formation of the Community 7-9 - through God-given patience 7f.
13 L 7:6-25 *supra*, 20f.	his own sin 17 possibility of abandoning the covenant 9 enemies 7f., 11f., 23f. - "despisers" 22	faithfulness to the covenant 8, 10, 19f. security 8f. everlasting glory, light, peace - ? his work has eternal significance 17f., 24f. ? messianic issue - Branch 19 (being a criterion 12)	God's grace and support alone 6-10, 16-19, - strengthening his spirit 8f. through God's revealed will, the Law 13-15, 20 and His spirit of holiness 6f. God's saving righteousness, צדקה, 19f.
11 J 6:3-36 *supra*, 22-24	? scorn, ruin, destruction 2f. the assembly of violence 5 a stormy experience 22-24	being taken into God's counsel along with the angels 5, 12f. hope 6 comfort 7	(those who reprove justly, to whom God opened his ear 4) repentance 6f. knowledge that there is hope for the repentant 6f.

TABLE I cont.

The author is saved

from	*to*	*through*
11 J cont.		entering the Community as a fortified city 24-29. ? founded on the truth 25, excluding strangers 27f.
8 H 4:5-5:4 *supra*, 24-26	enemies 22f sin of doubt, trembling at this 35	service of the cause of the covenant 5, 23f. (being a vehicle for God's mighty acts 8, 28, God's teachings 10, 27f.) attacking those who scorn him 22 being fortified 22, 36, 39	illumination 5, 23 leaning on God 22 and his compassion 36f. the memory of God's might and compassion 35f.

The following elements are stated to apply to men in general, or rather to the בני רצונו 32f.

	guilt from birth 29f.	knowing all God's works: his power and his mercy 32	only a spirit from God 31, making their way perfect 31f. This implies election 32f., 38 God's forgiveness, in putting away his wrath 37, through his צדקה 37
16 O/17 P 8:4-9:36 *supra*, 27-31	his enemies' charges: "mud" 8:14f., 9:3, 8f., 21, ? leading to his disease 9:1-9	teaching the Law to the Community 8:4, 16 destroying his enemies through his word 8:15, 20, cf. Jer. 1:10 rejoicing in his adversity, and in his enemies' scorn,	God's power and goodness, not man's 9:14-16, manifested in (a) his former trial 9:10-14 (b) God's treatment of him since his birth 9:29-36 - as predestinated 9:29-31 - as an instance of God's general care for his creatures 9:36 (a) displayed internally causing him to pray 9:10f., hope 11f., de-

TABLE I cont.

The author is saved

from	to	through
16 O/17 P cont.	as a chastisement 9:24-28	sire to obey 12, externally by physical preservation 11. Both constitute forgiveness 13.
	eternal glory, power, light, liberty and security 9:24-29.	(b) displayed internally teaching him the truth 31f., disposing him to the right through God's spirit 32, externally preserving him physically 30f., chastising him 33f., as a father 35f.
		God is his advocate as well as his judge 9:20-23, because He is as a father 33-36 since he chastises

TABLE II

The Community members are saved

from	to	through
5 E 3:5-18 *supra*, 15-17	death in "mother's" birth pangs 8, 10	tribulation of author: his "birth pangs" 7, 10
9 I 5:5-19 *supra*, 18	a covenant: a relationship of service and blessing 9	seeking the covenant 9 learning from the author 9 (contemplating God's might in respect of the author 15)
2 B 2:5-19 *supra*, 19	(sinning 10 ? through jealousy of the author 16) (being lost in error 19)	author's teaching of the truth 8f., 10, 13, 18. trial in connection with the author 13f.

TABLE II cont.

The Community members are saved

from	to	through

13 L
7:6-25
supra, 21

imbibing the milk of
the author's doctrine
20-22

11 J	guilt 8	being purified 8	obedience 8f.

11 J
6:3-36
supra, 22-24

guilt 8

being purified 8   obedience 8f.

being to God's   (repentance 14)
eternal and univers-
al glory 10-11 - as   God's kindness 8f.
a plant 15-17 - as
a light 18f.   God's instruction
                                      9f., 14
being united with
the angels צעה 13   ? not through a medi-
                                     ator 13f.
being a light and a
fire, consuming the
guilty 18f.

being "raised" to
this 34

8 H
4:5-5:4
supra, 26f.

error 25f.   standing before God   (power and wisdom of
                                 for ever 21   God's counsel 13)
the punishment
due to the men   direct access to   walking pleasing to
of deceit 20   God 24f.   God 21, 24

                              the eternal triumph being illuminated by
                              of their cause 25   the author's teaching
                                                                27
                              destroying all
                              transgressors 26f.   following this teach-
                                                                ing 24

16 O/17 P
8:4-9:36
supra, 27-31

(missing the   becoming the eter-   destruction of their
mystery 8:7-   nal restored Israel, enemies by the word of
11)   messianic community the author's mouth
                              8:4ff.   8:15-20
the destruction
decreed upon   becoming a source   author's Law teaching
the men of   of knowledge of the activity 8:21-26
falsehood   Law - water of life
8:15-20   8:8, 13f.   a thorough grounding
                                                               in the Law 8:7
                              being glorious
                              8:20, 22

From Table I it is evident that the author's sense of
Unheil developed as an increasing awareness of his own sin,
leading to a realization of universal sinfulness and the fact
that God alone can bring man's justification.

Salvation for the poet himself is seen throughout as founded upon God's power and goodness alone. In the final development of his conception of salvation these are operative through
God's preserving his life, instructing him in the truth and
disciplining him by chastisement. Even the latter is a sign
of God's love, for it is the activity of the Father. He is,
of course, also saved by his response to all this: patience
(including acceptance of the chastisement), obedience, repentance, trust. This response, however, is itself due to the
activity of God, who does not leave him to the devices of his
own guilty inclination, but strengthens him with His spirit
of holiness. A psychological as well as a theological account
is given of the reasons for the author's saving response, but
there is no suggestion that the latter can be reduced into
the terms of the former. Psychologically his response can be
seen as resulting from his awareness of God's dealings both
with mankind in general and in particular with the hymnist
himself during his past trials. Since this salvation is not
for all men, belief in election is implied throughout. All
this saving activity of God constitutes forgiveness and a
putting away of wrath. Probably even the chastisement is to
be seen as part of the forgiveness.[1]

The Founder's soteriology reached the form we have just
outlined by stages as indicated in the table below.

---

[1]   In the hymn in 1QS the same word (משפט) expresses both God's punishment
and His decree of justification. For a discussion of the term משפט with
the meaning "justification" see S. Schulz, "Zur Rechtfertigung aus Gnaden
in Qumran und bei Paulus," *Z. Theo. K.*, 56 (1959), p. 166. On Qumran
justification see also W. Grundmann, "The Teacher of Righteousness of
Qumran and the Question of Justification by Faith in the Theology of
the Apostle Paul," in *Paul and Qumran*, ed. J. Murphy-O'Connor, London,
1968, pp. 85-114.

TABLE III

Hymn	New elements	Old elements
10 J	a. God's power b. God's love c. man's need ("poor") d. knowledge of God's general dealings	
5 E	e. his own sufferings	a, b.
9 I	f. chastisement g. physical preservation by God h. the Law hidden by God in his heart (probably not only knowledge, but (i) disposition to obey). j. God's answering his cry	e.
2 B	k. formation of the Community l. patience	i.
13 L	m. spirit of holiness n. God's saving righteousness	a, b, h, i.
11 J	o. repentance (p) ? Community's reproof q. Community's exclusiveness	d, a, h.
8 H	r. trust s. memory of God's dealings t. election u. God's pardon (i.e. putting away wrath)	h, b, m, n, o.
16 O/17 P	v. legal imagery w. God as Father	a, b, d, e, f, g, h, i, j, m, r, s, t, u.

It is clear that the doctrine did not emerge ready-formed
out of the author's head, but was forged on the anvil of the
crises of his pilgrimage. Three main crises correspond to
three periods of new thinking about the means of salvation:
his rejection by the group of which he was formerly a member
(before 10 J), the formation of the Community (5 E and 9 I)
and his sickness (8 H and 16 O/17 P). During the first crisis
his sense of sin is absent and the hope of salvation centres

on his understanding of God's general dealings with the
needy. In the second crisis a sense of sin emerges and salvation is seen as involving the correction of his sinful inclination. During the third crisis there emerges a full spectrum
of "evangelical" piety: faith, election, forgiveness, justification. It is also at this final stage that the author sees
that God's salvation has put him in an impregnable position,
since he can rejoice even in his adversities.[1] By then he had
already experienced tribulation and God's forgiveness in it.

The Community members are represented as being saved from
sin, guilt and punishment through obedience to God by following the Teacher of Righteousness. At first they are learning
from the author, but later it is God who is said to be teaching them. This is because by then they were seen to belong
to the heavenly council.

G. THE SMALLER FOUNDER HYMNS

It remains to examine briefly hymns 3 C, 4 D, 7 G, and 12 K,
where the references to the author's enemies seem to indicate
that the author is the Founder, whose pilgrimage can be traced
in the hymns we have already considered.

In 3 C (2:20-30) and 4 D (2:31-38) the author is saved by
God from physical destruction by his enemies and from being
intimidated into abandoning the covenant (2:20-22, 31-33,
35f.). It is thus rather likely that these hymns were composed about the same time as 13 L, where the same themes also
occur. Here the means of salvation is God's love and guidance
(2:22f.) and the fall of his enemies into their own trap[2]
(2:29). This was all part of God's plan, so that he might
be glorified through the punishment of the wicked.[3]

---

[1] *Vid. supra*, p. 33.

[2] Cf. 4:19 in hymn 8 H (*supra*, p. 25) and Ps. 59:11-13.

[3] Cf. Exod. 9:14-16, 14:17f. The idea that God is glorified in his
punitive activity is an important O.T. theme: Lev. 10:2f., Num. 14:21-
23, Deut. 28:58-61, Josh. 7:19, Isa. 25:2f., Ezek. 28:22, 39:12f., 17-
21.

7 G is written at the end of one column and the beginning
of the next and is very fragmentary. One gathers merely that
he has been saved from his enemies by the power of God in
order that he might henceforth live in obedience to God.
What remains of 12 K describes the hymnist's distress at the
aspect of the sin which surrounds him, using imagery borrowed
from sickness and a storm at sea. In the lines which have
survived there is no mention of any salvation. It is likely
to have been composed at the beginning of the Founder's pilgrimage, about the same time as 10 J and 5 E.

Hymns 3 C and 4 D seem to contain allusions to the Community in 2:30 (praise of God in the congregation, a vow-
fulfilment activity typical in Old Testament piety for the
one who has experienced God's deliverance) and 2:37-39 (his
teaching activity in the Community). Nothing specific has
survived concerning the means of salvation for Community
members.

H. CONCLUSIONS ABOUT THE FOUNDER'S SOTERIOLOGY

These hymns are full of ideas about salvation, but atonement in the sense of a vicarious offering is totally absent.
The root כפר is used once only, and in that instance it is
God who is the subject and the verb means simply to forgive,
with overtones of the putting away of wrath. There is no
thought of a sacrifice as a ground for such "atonement". In
these hymns we are privileged to see the major tenets of the
Community being forged on the red-hot anvil of the Founder's
personal experience: covenant, election, עצה, God's spirit
of holiness, universal sinfulness, the acceptance of God's
punishment and the final destruction of the ungodly. This is
how his suffering became a source of salvation: by becoming
a source of truth. His disciples,therefore, are saved through
his teaching of this truth. There is no hint anywhere that
his sufferings have an objective value as a כופר, a ransom
or an expiation. God taught the Founder through his chastise-

ment and through the truth so taught saved him. The Founder
passes on this saving truth to the Community members, but they
may need chastisement too.[1]

---

[1] *Vid. supra*, p. 19.

CHAPTER II: SALVATION IN THE LEADER AND MEMBER HYMNS

A. THE LEADER HYMNS

The three hymns we have ascribed to a leader of the Community after the time of the Founder, 22 U, 25 X and 32 F[1], are of sufficient length and intelligibility to be treated as individual compositions for their soteriological contents. Since it is not possible to situate any of these compositions with reference to the pilgrimage of an individual author, there will be no attempt to arrange the hymns in chronological order. One has to be content simply to indicate in what respects each hymn differs from those by the Founder. The salvation ideas of each hymn will be considered in the context of each, since this gives a truer picture of the meaning than the collation of similar sayings from different contexts.[1] These hymns are rich in soteriological material, but poor in atonement sayings. By establishing the general salvation doctrine one can tell what room there may be for atonement as a means of salvation.[2]

Hymn 22 U (12:2-35) contains features similar to the hymn in 1QS: the idea of salvation as drawing near to God in the context of the Community,[3] the importance of praising God in time with the heavenly bodies which obey him perfectly,[4] the designation of the author as *maskîl*,[5] and the emphasis

----

[1] Cf. *supra*, p. 30, n. 3.

[2] The method proposed in this paragraph is also to be followed for those hymns by Community members which are long enough to be treated individually.

[3] 12:22f. Cf. 1QS 9:15, 11:13f.

[4] 12:4-11. Cf. 1QS 10:1-10. See too I Enoch 2:1-5:5; 21; 41:7ff.

[5] 12:11. Cf. 1QS 9:12. The term *maskîlîm* in Dan. 12:3 is used in connection with a corporate interpretation of the Suffering Servant figure in Isa. 53. This is clear not so much from the use of שכל in both passages, since this is not a very rare word, as from the use of the phrase "justify many" which occurs in conjunction with this. שכל hiph. in Daniel means "to be wise", or "to understand" with special reference to mysteries

on the depravity of mankind.[1] None of the first three of
these elements had been present in the Teacher of Righteousness hymns and even the fourth is now somewhat more stressed.

In 25 X (14:8-22) too there is the idea of drawing near in
the Community (14:13f., 18f.). As the author draws near to
God, his zeal against the wicked increases (14).[2] The author
had sworn an oath not to sin against God, and thus he had been
admitted into the community of the men of his assembly.[3] The
idea of predestination is implied, along with the division of
mankind into two lots: the righteous and the wicked (10-12,
15, 19). Since God has willed it so, the *maskîl* will love

---

and prophecies of the future. In Dan. 9:22 it clearly has the causative
sense "teach", "make to understand". In Isa. 52.:13 it bears the more
usual O.T. sense of "deal wisely", "prosper". It is a suitable term to
apply to a government functionary. Also justification is differently obtained in Daniel and Isaiah. Although in both cases the justification
involves the acquittal of "the many" in the great law suit which God holds
with his people, in Isaiah this is obtained through the Servant's bearing
the punishment of their iniquities, whereas in Daniel it is procured
through the teaching activity of the *maskîlîm* in the face of persecution
(11:33). Presumably the "many" gain acquittal by actually becoming righteous through hearkening to this instruction.

At Qumran we meet a Danielic type of usage for the hiph'îl of שכל (in
1QH 12:33 the verb has a causative sense, but there God is the subject
and the *maskîl* is the object). Yet it is not clear that we have an allusion in this hymn to Daniel, for there is no reference to a justifying
activity on the part of the *maskîl*. CD 20:18 ascribes a justifying function to each member of the Community, but this justification is to be
effected by the word of reproof. This, taken with the present hymn, may
indicate that the group thought of itself in terms of the *maskîlîm* of Dan.
11 and 12, but the fact that Daniel is presenting a re-interpretation of
the Isaianic Servant cannot be used as an argument for a Servant motif in
this hymn, since there is no proof that the author was aware that Daniel
was alluding to the Servant at this point. Cf. F.F. Bruce, *New Testament
Development*, pp. 90f.

Brownlee suggests that the Qumran *maskîlîm* taught in song (*The Meaning
of the Qumran Scrolls*, pp. 104-107).

[1] 12:24-32. Cf. 1QS 11:9-11, 20-22. For a comparison between the Qumran
view of man's extreme sinfulness and Paul's teaching see H. Braun, "Römer
7, 7-25 und das Selbstverständnis des Qumran-Frommen," *Z. Theo. K.*, 56
(1959), pp. 1-18, also S. Schulz, *op. cit.*

[2] This is a sign that this hymn is not from the Founder, who had suffered
at the hand of the wicked at the beginning of his pilgrimage and did not
need to learn to hate them.

[3] 14:17f. Delcor (*op. cit.*, p. 264) sees here a clear reference to the
initiatory oath of the Essenes (cf. Josephus, *Wars*, II 8, 7).

and hate every man according to God's acceptance or rejection
of each.[1]

Hymn 32 F[1] is written on the extremely fragmentary column
18. Not one complete line of text has survived. The Leader's
Unheil is termed "snares of judgement" (Mansoor) in line 25.
Since the theme is the speaker's unworthiness before God, it
is God's judgement that is being referred to. A comparison
with 3:26-28 (6 F) makes it probable that the whole phrase
"snares of judgement" refers to the eschatological outpouring
of the wrath of God of which the hymnist has received a fore-
taste through the bitter experience of his former association
with the enemies of the Community.[2] In the Community's thinking the theme of eschatological wrath was already implicit in
the birth travail imagery used by the Founder to describe his
own experiences.[3] This hymn contains the first clear statement that salvation for the members of the Community is
through the Leader's words of reproof (12f.), not just through
his teaching in general.[4] It is also to be noted that in
lines 14f. this activity is described in terms borrowed from
Isa. 61:1-2, a passage recalling the Servant Songs.

B. THE MEMBER HYMNS

It can be asserted with a large degree of confidence that
the Leader hymns were composed after the Founder hymns, since
the Leaders were presumably the successors of the Founder.
The same cannot be asserted of the Member hymns which are now
to be considered, since there would be members from the very
beginning. No attempt will be made to treat the Member hymns
in chronological order, since a *Sitz im Leben* criterion is
not available here as it was for the Founder hymns. 6 F will

---

[1] God's will is righteous and is accepted as such. When God finally
destroys the wicked, this righteousness צדקה will be manifest to all
creation (16). The use of צדקה here, a word usually reserved for God's
saving righteousness, to express God's punitive justice, is evidence of
the poet's total acceptance of all that God wills. Cf. *supra*, p. 9, n. 3.

[2] Cf. 3:24f.

[3] Hymn 5 E, 3:7-18.

[4] But see *supra*, p. 19 on 2:13f.

be treated first, since it has affinities with 32 F[1], the
hymn just discussed. The rest will be treated in the order
in which they appear in the scroll.

Hymn 6 F (3:19-36) is notable for its vivid description of
the eschatological river of fire from which the author has
been saved. This river had already overflowed its banks and
was rampaging throughout the world (3:29f.). Ultimately it
would destroy everything, reaching even to the deepest hell
(31f.). This fiery stream is called "the torrents of Belial",
but probably this just means "the torrents of wickedness".[1]
At first this is simply an image expressing the dangers inherent in the poet's former association with the wicked, described in lines 24-28, but in line 31 he declares that this
river of fire will destroy the whole universe. It is the work
of God and of the angels (34-36). The author has been saved
from great sin in connection with his former association with
the reprobate.[2] God has rescued him from the "Sheol of Abaddon" and set him upon an "eternal height" (19f.). He is now
united with the angels and a member of their army (21-23).
This supernal and infernal imagery may be borrowed from the
sphere of the after-life ideas of the second century B.C.,[3]
but it is clear that what is being described is the present
condition of the author. He has been delivered from a hell
on earth and has taken refuge in the heaven upon earth, which
is the Community. This hell upon earth, however, is going to
destroy the whole universe. It should be no source of sur-
prise that this destruction is seen as a manifestation of the
wrath of God (34), since Hebrew thought was very familiar with
the idea that the enemies of God could be the instruments of
his righteous wrath (e.g. Isa. 10:5ff.). What is perhaps more
puzzling is the fact that in one of the Founder hymns (11 J,
6:17-19), the river of fire issues from the Community, whilst

---

[1] So Delcor, *op. cit.*, p. 130 and cf. p. 37.

[2] Following Delcor's rendering of חללי□ in line 25. Whereas this word
refers to the victims of the wicked in Ps. 10:8, 10, 14, it refers to the
wicked themselves in 1QH 4:25, 35.

[3] Mansoor suggests that the Sheol of Abaddon may refer to one of the
hollow places of I Enoch 22 where the spirits of the wicked are slain.

here it flows from the Community's enemies. Was the group's
thinking on this theme totally confused?[1] The solution to
the problem probably lies in the realization that the river
of fire does not symbolize the enemy so much as the conflict
itself. Hence either of the combatants can be spoken of as
its source, whether Belial or the righteous angels and their
allies in the Community.[2]

Hymn 1 A (1:1-39) sets the key-note for the expression of
the Community's piety in the rest of the scroll. It stresses
the unworthiness of man and the sovereignty of God in most
uncompromising terms. Man is the source of all wickedness
and God of all righteousness (26f.). Even the poet's words
are known and decreed by God before he utters them (23f., 27-
29). This includes not only his pronouncement of the mysteries
which God had revealed to him (21), but also his praise (29f.)
and even his confession of sin (25f.). He is thus utterly
bankrupt before God. It is difficult to conceive how the
ideas of merit and supererogation could emerge from a milieu
in which this kind of piety was the norm.[3]

This hymn has certain affinities with the discourse on the
two spirits in 1QS 3:13ff., but here there is no explicit
dualism.[4] God has created every spirit and fixed their judgement according to all their works (1:8f.), but even this
judgement seems to be something manifested in time (16-19).
Indeed, there is no final judgement in this hymn. We are
either to assume that the human race will continue for ever,
or that the term "eternal generations" means simply "until the

---

[1] Ps. 18 is obviously in the background (so Delcor, *op. cit.*, p. 131),
but there God's wrath, penetrating even to the foundations of the earth
(verse 15), was being activated in order to rescue the psalmist from the
rivers of Belial (verse 4). Part of the appearance of confusion here may
be caused by the fusion of the idea of God's ubiquitous wrath with that
of the Torrents of Belial.

[2] Cf. Dan. 10:13, 20f., 12:1. This interpretation would accord with
Mansoor's rendering of lines 35f: "the battle of the mighty ones of heaven
shall be waged abroad in the universe."

[3] *Pace* Bruce, *New Testament Development*, p. 91.

[4] Dupont-Sommer, however, introduces an explicit dualism here by the way
he fills the lacunæ (*The Essene Writings*, pp. 202f.).

end of the world".[1]

In hymn 19 R (10:14-11:2) hardly a complete line has survived, but the gist is fairly clear. There are two new
points: the judgement of the angels (34)[2] and the fact that
he does not trust in riches for salvation (22f.). It is uncertain whether the hymnist's salvation is a purely spiritual
matter, for it is not clear whether the material blessings,
mentioned in lines 24-28, are to be enjoyed by the author,
or whether they are simply a list of the things desired by a
worldly person. It is possible that he expects to receive
these things because of God's faithfulness, though he has
not set his heart upon them.

In hymn 20 S most of the lines are well preserved (11:3-14).
Here we meet language which presents life in the Community
as an end of salvation and not merely as a means (11:11f.).
Closely linked with this end is the reception of God's revelation (4, 9). The reason why membership in the Community can
be seen as an end in itself is that it already involves union
with the angelic hosts (11:13). The imagery belongs to the
council chamber: the revelation is God's "counsel" (סוד).
There is also something of temple imagery present: the author
has been purified and sanctified so as to be fitted for this
holy association (10f.). Through this association he will
participate in the renewal which God is to bring about, for
he knows what is to come and rejoices in it already (13f.).[3]
This is not exactly new creation, but rather participation in
the new things which God is about to do. This thought is already familiar from the Old Testament (Isa. 42:9, 43:19, 48:6).

---

[1] "Eternal generations" cannot mean an eternity beyond this world since
in line 18 it is connected with the idea of descendants.

[2] This idea may also be present in the Leader hymn 22 U (12:29-31), but
there a lacuna makes the meaning uncertain. See too I Enoch 11-15, where
the fallen angels are condemned to eternal punishment.

[3] For a discussion of the difficulties in connection with the text see
Holm-Nielsen, op. cit., pp. 187f., n. 27. The present interpretation is
based on the only elements in the reading of which we can be reasonably
certain: עם כול נהיה and an attempt to interpret this in parallel with
what follows, "and with all those who have knowledge in the community of
rejoicing."

The reference to the raising of the "worms of the dead" in line 12 does not necessarily imply a literal resurrection.[1]

As for the means of salvation, this hymn introduces a strong emphasis on God as the only source of all saving characteristics (7-9): truth, righteousness (צדקה), knowledge, strength, chastisement[2] and pardon. The root of all these is the goodness of God (6f.), which he has exercised for the sake of his own glory (10).

21 T (11:15-36) is remarkable for its concern for the suffering of the entire universe and its hope for an end of all evil. The tone is almost universalistic.[3] The poet has emerged from a time of intense sadness at the contemplation of the sin and suffering in the world. He declares his intention to keep up this mourning until all evil is abolished (19-22). This causes him to think how he <u>will</u> praise God along with all creation (23-27). Meditation on this leads him to bless God <u>now</u> for giving him an understanding of what He is going to do (27-36).[4] In the course of this worship he becomes conscious of his sinful condition and asks for cleansing (30f.). Clearly he is no longer mourning the evil of the world but rejoicing in the goodness of God, and this change has been brought about by the contemplation of what God is going to do.

---

[1] *Vid. supra*, pp. 23f.

[2] This is at least potentially saving. Cf. 1:33 where an almost identical phrase is used.

[3] For an assessment of the anti-universalistic tendencies of Qumran see Carmignac, *op. cit.*, p. 386 and "La théologie de la souffrance dans les Hymnes de Qumrân," *Rev. Qum.*, 3 (1961-2), pp. 373f.

[4] Cf. 11:13f, in hymn 20 S, *supra*, p. 46. The universalistic tone of the present hymn raises the question of the Community's belief in eternal punishment. Perhaps they believed in the total destruction of the wicked, viz. annihilation. It is theoretically possible that there was such whole-hearted acceptance of all God's judicial decisions as righteous that all his punishments, even his eternal penalty, were seen as an unmitigated good (certainly the "battlements" motif in the inter-testamental literature is to be seen in this way rather than as a carnal gloating: I Enoch 27, 62:9, 97:2, 108:14f., Ass. Mos. 10 - though Jub. 23:30 is a possible exception), but the language here clearly implies an end of suffering, though this may be limited to the redeemed creation to which the author already belongs. Though the hymn laments the suffering caused by sin, there is no lamentation for the suffering of the day of wrath.

Column 13, on which hymn 23 V is written, does not contain
a single complete line and most of the lines have only three
or four complete words. Nevertheless, the main points are
clear. The new elements are the materialistic terms used to
express the end of salvation and the view of salvation in
terms of spirits.[1] One may also note that in line 19 God's
צדק has a saving quality related to his keeping his promises
so that his word can be relied upon. This should warn us
against insisting on too great a difference between God's
saving righteousness (צדקה) and the ordinary concept of his
justice (צדק, משפט) which could include punitive justice. In
any case, there is at least one instance where צדקה means punitive justice in 1QH[2] and in 1QS 11 משפט means "justification". It is possible that the thought of justification is
present here too, expressed by the verb צדק in lines 16f.,
which Mansoor translates, "Only through Thy goodness / May a
man be righteous . . ." It is not clear, however, whether
this righteousness of man is primarily the practice of righteousness or a judicial standing before God. Probably both are
involved, for the thought here seems to be a development of
17 P which expresses hope in God's goodness, since no man can
be righteous before God (9:14f.). In 17 P it is clear that
the author is to be made "righteous" by God's pleading his
cause (9:23)[3] and by God's chastisement improving him practically (9:23-26). The idea of a new creation is explicitly
stated in 11f.[4]

Hymn 27 Z (15:9-26) is noteworthy for its uncompromising
statement of double predestination, but God, who thus pre-
destinates is no mere arbitrary despot.[5] He is the object

---

[1] Salvation results in pleasures and long life (17f.). Cf. 10:24-28 and
supra, p. 46. Man is to be saved from (or in spite of) the dominion of a
perverted spirit (15f.) through the enlightenment of a spirit from God (19).

[2] *Vid. supra*, p. 43 n. 1. Another reference to a saving צדק is possibly
to be found in 11:18.

[3] Presumably this would be before God's own tribunal! Cf. Rom. 8:33f.

[4] Cf. *supra*, pp. 46f.

[5] For somewhat more arbitrary predestination ideas cf. 4Q 181 f 1:5
(*Discoveries*, V, pp. 79f.).

of spontaneous love and worship (10). Salvation for the
elect is in two stages. The first is a life of holiness
in this world, the second eternal salvation and peace (16).
The first stage is called "the time of favour" (15). Presumably this period is to extend until "the day of slaughter"
(17), when it would be too late to repent.[1] The holiness of
the first period consists of faithfulness to the covenant
(15), perfect love and obedience towards God (10, 11, 15)
and submission to the Community's discipline (11). It is a
time when the glory of the elect is raised above all flesh.[2]
This holiness in the elect is effected through God's sovereign
control over his spirit and his ways (12-15, 23f.). The
statement in line 24 that God will not accept a bribe or a
כופר is probably related to the thought expressed in 19 R
that the member does not trust in wealth for his salvation
(10:22f.).[3]

29 C[1] (17:9-15) does not contain a single complete line.
The author would appear to have been saved from the fire,
from Sheol and from God's judgement against his transgressions,
including his sinful thoughts (10-13). His salvation is ef-

---

[1] For the "repent in time" motif in relation to the approach
of the pre-messianic woes cf. Syb. Or. III, 624 ff.

[2] Taking ותרם (16f.) as consecutive to הכינותו (15): "From the womb Thou
didst establish him for the time of favour . . . and Thou hast raised
his glory above all flesh." Mansoor translates ותרם by a future, but he
is willing to see a breakdown of the older *waw* constructions in the Hymns
(*The Thanksgiving Hymns*, p. 22). The interpretation we have adopted (so
too Delcor, Dupont-Sommer, Holm-Nielsen and Eduard Lohse, *Die Texte aus
Qumran*, Darmstadt, 1964, p. 167) may be compared with Eph. 1:3, 2:1-10,
where the faithful are declared to be raised already into heavenly places
(see too Delcor, *Les Hymnes*, p. 271). If Mansoor's rendering is right,
one would have after-life doctrine apart from resurrection. If מבשר were
translated "from flesh", however, a resurrection would be implied.

[3] Qumran seems to have hesitated to believe in a כופר as a substitutionary atonement. Although Job 33:24-26 envisages such a possibility, 11Q
Targ. Job, *ad loc.* probably eliminates the concept. See Pierre Grelot's
reconstruction in his review of *Le Targum de Job de la Grotte XI de Qumrân*, edd. J.P.M. Van der Ploeg and A.S. Van der Woude, Leiden, 1971: *Rev.
Qum.* 8 (1972), p. 111.

fected by God's pardoning activity (כפר, 12),[1] seen under the
image of casting away sin (15), and results in the survival
of his posterity and in long life (14f.). This state of
affairs is called "all the glory of Adam", a phrase which occurs also in the Rules (1QS 4:23, CD 3:20) and exemplifies
the emphasis on Adam's loss of immortality rather than as the
one through whom sin entered the world. This is the usual
emphasis in the earlier inter-testamental literature.[2]

C. SUMMARY OF THE SALVATION IDEAS OF THE MAJOR 1QH HYMNS

All the major Founder, Leader and Member hymns have now been
considered and the leading elements in their soteriology can
be tabulated.

TABLE IV

1. *Unheil*

    externals (e.g. enemies, disease)

    human weakness

    error

    sin   - sinful inclination

                      - guilt (guilty feelings, relationship of guilt
                       before God)

    coming punishment

---

[1] In spite of the lacunæ it is probable that God is the subject here
and that the verb is followed by בעד governing the sins to be forgiven.
This would indicate the influence of Exod. 32:30 as in 4Q Dib. Ham. 2:9
(*vid. supra*, p. 11), but the change of subject from Moses to God shows
that Exod. 32 has been interpreted in the light of its sequel in 34:7,
where God is proclaimed as the one who is merciful and forgives. Thus
in 1QH 17:12 Moses, instead of atoning for Israel, proclaims that God
atones. The principle behind this interpretation is that, if man is said
to forgive, this means that he proclaims God's forgiveness (cf. 4QNab 1:4,
vid. supra, p. 12).

[2] This literature emphasises the events of Gen. 6 in relation to the
introduction of sin. Cf. I Enoch 10:8, 19:1, chs. 24f., 32:3ff., Test.
Lev. 18:10, Jub. 3, 4:30, 10:1-5. The "sin unto death" in Jubilees seems
to result in loss of posterity, e.g. 21:21ff., end of ch. 26. Ecclus. 17
has no doctrine of the Fall whatsoever, but cf. 25:24.

By the time of 4 Ezra it is Adam who introduces sin into the world:
see 3:21, 4:30, 7:46-48 (116-118). See too Rom. 5:12. Wisdom takes Adam's
Fall for granted (Wisd. 10:1).

TABLE IV cont.

2. Results of salvation

    to gain   - externals (e.g. triumph over enemies)

                      - a relationship with God (e.g. acceptance)

                      - knowledge of God and his counsel

                      - an internal experience (e.g. peace, joy)

                      - an eternal destiny

    to give   - ethical obedience to God

                      - glory to God

3. Means of salvation

    God's might

    God's love

    God's election

    God's faithfulness (including צדקה)

    God's forgiveness

    God's instruction

    God's work in the heart

    God's chastisement, discipline (including that mediated by the Community)

    God's physical preservation

    man's patience

    man's knowledge of God's dealings

    man's trust in God

    man's repentance

    man's spirit of holiness received from God

    man's obedience

    the activity of the Community (teaching, reproving, excluding sinners)

    the protection of the angels

These elements, however, are mostly manifested with differing degrees of emphasis in the different types of hymn material. The following table summarizes our findings.

TABLE V

1. *Unheil*

   a. For Founder in Founder hymns

   Very concerned with deliverance from externals, especially enemies. Increasing sense of sin.

   b. For Members in Founder hymns

   No concern about deliverance from externals or from human weakness. This is probably because the Founder himself sought and found refuge from these in the Community (viz. in the Members).

   c. For Leader in Leader hymns

   No mention of externals. This is probably because he has emerged from within the Community.

   d. For Members in Leader hymns

   Nothing is stated.

   e. For Members in Member hymns

   The idea of coming punishment, absent in a., is now frequent. The theme of human weakness is stronger, but the stress on error has disappeared. Is this a doctrinally "safe" membership in a Community which has lost something of its first enthusiasm?

2. Results of salvation

   a. Founder in Founder hymns

   Not until the Community is formed does he see salvation as a triumph over his enemies.
   All the major ideas in 1QH about the end of salvation are already present in the Founder hymns.

   b. Members in Founder hymns

   Here triumph over enemies is a factor, but it is linked with the thought of glory for God and the Community, not with fear of enemies.
   Not all the major ideas are present as yet, but they are implicit in the association between the Members and the Founder (see a.).

   c. Leader in Leader hymns

   Every important element is represented.

   d. Members in Leader hymns

   Too little material to make any judgement about tendency.

   e. Members in Member hymns

   All elements are reasonably well represented.

TABLE V cont.

3. Means of salvation

    a. Founder in Founder hymns

    For the development *vid. supra*, pp. 37f.
    All the major ideas have already appeared.

    b. Members in Founder hymns

    There is great stress on knowledge and a total absence of for-
    giveness.
    The Founder is a means of salvation in all except 11 J, where the
    Community's reproof is a means of salvation for the Founder.

    c. Leader in Leader hymns

    Heavy stress on knowledge. No mention of forgiveness.

    d. Members in Leader hymns

    As for c.
    The discipline of the Community is coming into view.
    No mention of forgiveness.

    e. Members in Member hymns

    Forgiveness is now coming into prominence. It is often seen as
    a cleansing.
    The discipline of the Community is not mentioned, even God's
    discipline is little stressed (cf. a.).
    Election has gained in importance since a.
    Physical preservation is no longer an element in salvation (cf. a.
    and b.).
    The activity of the angels is a new factor here.

D. SHORT AND FRAGMENTARY MEMBER HYMNS

   The hymns so far considered have been long enough for the
introduction of a variety of soteriological elements in each.
In the shorter and more fragmentary hymns to which we now turn
these elements are almost entirely governed by the *genre* or
type of composition in each case.

   14 M (7:26-33) is a song of thanksgiving for enlightenment
in spite of the author's unworthiness. This involves, of
course, God's forgiveness. The hymn is noteworthy for its
thoroughly biblical argument for eternal-life doctrine: since
God is eternal, his ways are eternal (31).[1]

------

[1] Cf. Emil Brunner, *The Christian Doctrine of Creation and Redemption,*
Dogmatics, II, London, 1952, pp. 68f.

15 N (7:34-8:3) is a hymn of thanksgiving for God's forgiveness and election. It is quite fragmentary. 18 Q (9:37-
10:12) celebrates God's sovereignty. Salvation is by election, from human weakness, to knowledge of God's secret. 24 W
seems to be a description of the moral qualities of the Community members, but it is too fragmentary to discern any soteriological significance in these (14:1-7).

26 Y (14:23-27) is a prayer of thanksgiving for the use of
one who has entered the Community. It proclaims that God par-
dons the repentant and favours them with the spirit of knowledge so that they love God and hate iniquity.

28 A[1] (16:3-19) is not a short hymn, but unfortunately no
line remains intact. It seems to be a prayer of penitence by
a new Member or one who is to be re-instated. The realization of the power and love of God had encouraged the author
to pray for strengthening by God's spirit of holiness (1-7).
God had bestowed this spirit upon him and by this spirit he
had "softened the face" of God (11f.). Clearly God takes
pleasure in those qualities of a man which He himself has
placed within him. Thus God was linked with the spirit of
his servant and with all his works (14). All this illustrates
the forgiving character of God who goes so far as to "repent"
of the evil intended towards man, if only there is whole-
hearted contrition (16-18).

30 D[1] (17:17-25) is another hymn of penitence thanking God
for forgiveness and for a spirit of obedience. Very little
has survived of 31 E[1] (17:26f.). What there is simply expresses thanks for the gift of God's spirit of holiness.

These hymns display no particular "trend" beyond what can
be explained in terms of the *genre* of each. There is a noteworthy stress on "spirit" in the penitential hymns 26 Y, 28 A[1],
30 D[1], 31 E[1]. Similarly, in the Fragments, we have the re-
currence of typical themes with frequent mention of the spirit.
The verb נכפר occurs in f 2:13. The probable reconstruction
of the immediate context gives, "Thou hast sprinkled upon him
the spirit of thy holiness[1] to atone for guilt (לכפר

---
[1] Cf. 7:7 and 17:26 in Mansoor's translation, also f 2:10.

אשמה)‎‎‎."[1] This is a development of the thought of 7:7 (in
13 L, a Founder hymn) that God's gift of the spirit prevented
the author from falling into sin at a time of trial, but perhaps it has more affinities with 16:11f.,[2] where the spirit
is a means of "softening the face" of the Deity. The link
between the use of the verb כפר and the idea of God's abandoning his wrath has already been noted.[3]

E. FORGIVENESS AND ATONEMENT IN 1QH

In 1QH forgiveness is not the only means of salvation. It
is even possible for a whole section of this literature (the
Leader hymns) to speak of salvation without mentioning forgiveness, almost exclusively in terms of God's election, instruction and work in the heart.[4] If God does this for the
unworthy, He has already forgiven him, of course, but the
author does not feel the need to make this explicit. This
may be due to lack of stress on the need for salvation (*Unheil*) in 25 X and 32 F[1]. It is also possible that 22 U,
which seems to evince a sense of *Unheil* (12:21), originally
contained some allusion to forgiveness where there is now a
lacuna. In the Member hymns we meet once more the idea of
forgiveness, but here it is grounded upon God's taking pleasure in what he himself produces in man's heart and life
through the spirit which he has bestowed upon him. It is
clear that the experience of the Founder is being appropriated
by the Members. No direct line of development from the Founder through the Leader to the Members can be insisted on, only
the general primacy of the Founder hymns. Atonement, as the
objective basis of forgiveness, is here to be equated with
this spirit of holiness from God, and nothing more (16:11,

---

[1] The construction of כפר with sin as the direct object is the "Isaianic
usage" (see Appendix B, *infra*, pp. 125, 127f.). This construction occurs
also in 1QH 4:37 (*supra*, p. 26).

[2] Hymn 28 A[1], *vid. supra*, p. 54.

[3] *Supra*, p. 10.

[4] The fact that these *Maskil* hymns have so little to say about forgiveness surely indicates that in spite of Dan. 12:3 the *maskîlîm* and the
Servant of Isa. 53:11 were not identified in Qumran thinking.

f 2:13).[1] It is clearly an atonement for the person possess-
ing the spirit and for no one else. There is no mention of
the works produced by this spirit as works of supererogation.
Indeed the works themselves are not really counted as merits
at all even for the salvation of the doer, for the utter unworthiness of the author is greatly stressed in the immediate
contexts of both passages concerned. He is simply saying
that he has nothing whatsoever to plead before God except
what is after all God's gift to him: his spirit of holiness.[2]

---

[1] *Vid. supra*, pp. 54f.

[2] It is possible that even this interpretation gives too much colour to
the verbs concerned. Perhaps חלה פני means simply "entreat" (cf. Ps.
119:58) and כפר "cleanse" (cf. Prov. 16:6). If so, the words would be
dead metaphors. It is probable, however, that they still retain the
flavour of averting wrath. *Vid. infra*, p. 124.

CHAPTER III: ATONEMENT PASSAGES IN 1QS[1]

A. 1QS 3:6-12

1QS is a rule presented as a programme. It purports to
give regulations for the life of a Community which is to be
constituted when certain moral conditions obtain amongst
those who would be its members.[2]

The reasons for this Community's existence are hinted at
in connection with the doctrine of the spirits of light and
of darkness. The struggle of these two is universal, but
God has decreed an end to the spirit of darkness. Then
everything which is of falsehood will be destroyed and those
whose way of life is perfect will inherit the glory of Adam.
The Community exists so that those who freely offer themselves may be ready for this inheritance. These are the
people who take sides with God in the dispute which he has
with the entire human race.[3] This means that they accept
God's judgement both upon themselves and upon the whole of
sinful mankind.

The Community Rule opens by declaring that the Community
exists for righteousness. This involves perfect obedience
to the divine ordinances on the part of those who join and
a sharing of God's attitudes towards men and things. Their
loves and hatreds must be identical with God's (1:1-18).
There follow prescriptions for the blessing of God and of
the faithful as well as for the cursing of the wicked (1:18-
2:18). This includes the prayer that God may not forgive

---

[1] 1QS 8:15b-9:11, a section which is judged by Starcky to have been
added later, since it is not present in 4QS[e], will be examined in a
later chapter.

[2] It is clear, however, from the amount of detailed regulation, that
the Community was probably already functioning at the time of writing.

[3] CD 1:2.

(כפר) the latter.[1] Membership of the Community involves
entering into a covenant[2] before God, which is to be renewed
annually by all the members, each in the order of his spiritual standing (1:16, 2:19-25). No one is to be admitted whose
motives are not perfect, since such a person cannot be purified by atonement rituals or ablutions, as long as he per-
sists in a rebellious attitude. Furthermore, he contaminates
the rest of the Community by his presence (2:25-3:6).[3]

The passage under consideration then explains why (כי א,
3:6) such a person will remain unclean. It is because he
has been excluded from the Community, hence from the context
where the spirit of God's counsel is operative. "The spirit
of the counsel of the truth of God" (line 6) is available
only "in the Community of His counsel" (line 5).[4] This whole
section constitutes a strong warning to any who may fall away
through revolting against the Community's discipline. The
Community was bound in spiritual self-defence to excommunicate
such a person. Once away from the Community, he would be away
from the means of grace and "unable to repent".[5] There is no
concern to restore such renegades to salvation, only to maintain the Community as a means of salvation by excluding apostates and to preserve those who were still members from falling away and being lost.

---

[1]   2:8. This, however, was perfectly compatible with sharing God's attitude to everyone. *Vid.* I Enoch 13f., where Enoch's prayer for forgiveness for the Watchers was not according to the will of God. For a discussion of the meaning of כפר in this line *vid. infra*, pp. 70-73.

[2]   This refers to the covenant embodied in CD or in an earlier recension
of CD.

[3]   Cf. the idea that the exclusiveness of the Community is a source of
salvation, 1QH 6:27f., *supra*, p. 22. At Qumran, sin and its influence
seem to have been thought of as a kind of uncleanness (cf. Num. 31:15-
24), so that ritual ablutions were used for penitents and not merely for
those who were Levitically unclean (1QS 3:8-11).

[4]   "Counsel" still seems to be the meaning of עצה in 1QS, rather than
"council". The phrase "Community of His counsel" means the Community
where God's decisions are heard, understood and heeded. "The spirit
of the counsel of the truth of God" is the capacity and inclination to
understand and obey these decisions.

[5]   3:1 as rendered by Wernberg-Møller.

Atonement is mentioned here alongside of cleansing as a
synonym, as Ringgren has remarked.[1] This has been facilitated
by the use of "cleansing" as a metaphor for putting away sin,
but atonement, even here, is not merely the removal of the
sin, but the ground of man's acceptance by God (3:11). This
ground is said to be the spirit of obedience (6-8). The idea
is similar to that expressed in 1QH 16:11f. and f 2:13,[2] but
at this place it is not mentioned that the atoning spirit
comes from God himself. The reason is the difference between
the two types of discourse. 1QH is praise, and the stress is
on God's goodness. This passage is a kind of homily, where
the stress is on man's responsibility.

Ablutions and rituals of atonement are effective only when
the attitude is right (8-11). The water of purification (מי
נדה) mentioned in line 9 is probably the same as that described in Num. 19. It was produced by mixing with the ashes of
a heifer. The ritual associated with this was entirely performed outside of the temple precincts and there seems to be
no reason why the Qumranites should not have had their own
מי נדה unless their priests objected to the recognition of
the defiled Jerusalem temple that would be implied by com-
pliance with Num. 19:4. The מי דוכי also mentioned later
in line 9 was probably some cleansing ritual developed in
the Community itself. The בכנופי of line 11 may refer to
these two kinds of oblations or some other rite.[3]

There remains the question whether the meaning of this
clause in line 11 should be determined by that of the following clause, "and it shall be for him a covenant of an everlasting community", which would seem to be an echo of Num.
25:13, "and it shall be unto him, and to his seed after him,
the covenant of an everlasting priesthood; because he was
jealous for his God, and made atonement for the children of
Israel", where Phinehas was stated to have atoned for Israel

---

[1] Op. cit., pp. 121-123.

[2] Vid. supra, pp. 54f. Our passage shares with 1QH f 2:13 also the
"Isaianic usage" of the verb.

[3] It seems to refer back to the בכנופים of line 4 which had to do with
atonement rituals. Line 11 means, "Then he will be accepted with an

by taking God's attitude towards sin and acting accordingly.
The Community frequently regarded itself as the Phinehas of
its own generation, even to the point of condemning and punishing the wicked,[1] and this thought is probably in the background in the present context. Though the language here does
not closely parallel that of Num. 25:13, it certainly echoes
it. The intention is to indicate that the truly repentant
person can take his place in the Community after the proper
rituals, and the Phinehas function of the Community is briefly reflected in language coloured by the Numbers passage.
Repentance in this context is itself something of a Phinehas
function, since it is choosing God's will and displaying his
attitude in resisting contamination for Israel.

B. 1QS 5:1-7

   This passage, though immediately preceded by the discourse
on the two spirits (3:13-4:26), seems to represent a new beginning, - or rather a false beginning, since the promise of
a rule made in line 1 has to be taken up again in line 7, because of the mass of qualifying phrases introduced. The passage abounds in constructions with ל plus the infinitive. It
is not a rule, in spite of the promise of line 1, since we
find ordinary imperfectives rather than a string of ל constructions when the promised rule is finally introduced in
lines 7ff. The present passage is an expression of the
character of the Community members (1-3) and of the Community's reason for existence (3-7).[2] The way in which the
atonement, mentioned in lines 6f., is connected with all this
depends upon the interpretation or emendation of the puzzling
ונאם in line 5.

---

atonement ritual pleasing to God" not "then his submissive attitude will
be accepted as an atonement". We take ירצה as a niph'al, following
Wernberg-Møller. The subject is masculine, not neuter.

[1] *Vid. infra*, pp. 66f., 74, 87, 102f.

[2] It would seem that the ל constructions here usually express purpose
and that each is subordinate to the preceding, since they are not linked
by means of ו (cf. 1:1ff.).

(a) According to Brownlee,[1] ואאם stands for אלוהי האלוהים
ואדוני האדונים "the God of gods and Lord of lords." He sees
the following advantages over other theories which involve
an emendation of the text.

i.   It is explainable in terms of the allusion to Deut. 10:
16f. and 30:6f.

ii. God is a more appropriate subject for the verbs which
follow, and especially for "atone[2] for all those who offer
themselves" since this avoids the difficult conception of
the Community atoning for itself.

iii. Surrogates for the divine name occur elsewhere in the
Scrolls, for example CD 15:1.

The following points may be added to the arguments given
by Brownlee.

iv. In Deut. 21:8, Isa. 22:14 and Ezek. 16:63, the only instances where כפר is followed by ל governing the person to
be forgiven, it is God who is the subject of the action of
the verb.[3]

v.   This interpretation involves no emendation, and it is
doubtful whether any of the emendations suggested can explain
how the supposed mistake arose or was perpetuated. The scribe
has clearly written ואאם not ויאאם[4] and he shows no sign of

---

[1] *The Dead Sea Manual of Discipline, Translation and Notes*, New Haven,
Conn., 1951, p. 19, n. 18 and pp. 49f.

[2] The subordination of this verb to the preceding clause does not pre-
vent God from being the subject according to the sense.

[3] See Lyonnet, "De notione expiationis," *Verbum Domini*, Rome, 37 (1959),
p. 334. Ezek. 16:63 is probably the background here. Cf. "eternal covenant" 5:5 with Ezek. 16:60. The Ezekiel context is Yahweh's forgiveness
of Israel after she has borne the punishment of Exile.

[4] Whereas this scribe often writes *waw* in a manner indistinguishable
from *yod*, in this case he has a curve at the bottom such as he does not
have for his *yod*s. *Vid. The Dead Sea Scrolls of St. Mark's Monastery*,
ed. by Millar Burrows, John C. Trever and William H. Brownlee, Vol. II,
fascicle 2, New Haven, Conn., 1951, *ad loc.* and *passim*, also the coloured
photographs reproduced in *Scrolls from Cave I*, ed. John C. Trever, Jerusalem, 1972, p. 135 and *passim*.

fatigue in this column.[1]

Against Brownlee's view is the fact that he has to take
the infinitival phrases with ל as almost equivalent to main
verbs. These phrases, which are very frequent in the Scrolls,
are often translated as finite verbs, but this is presumably
simply part of the process of reducing the longer sentences
in which they occur to a series of shorter ones. A similar
construction does occur, however, in the Old Testament in
Isa. 38:20, יהוהׁ להושיעני, where the R.V. translates, "The
LORD is *ready* to save me." Probably we have a similar sense
here: "God is ready to circumcise . . . the foreskin of the
inclination . . . so as to establish a true foundation . . .
in order to atone for all who offer themselves".[2]

(b) Wernberg-Møller has followed M. Burrows in emending
ואאם to האשם or אשם which is to be taken with the preceding
words, "his guilty inclination". This would have the advantage of making the ומחשבה יצרו אשם here parallel to the ומחשבות
יצר אשמה of CD 2:16. This emendation would yield the following meaning for lines 3-7.-

The decisions of the Community authorities shall be para-
mount so that the requirements of Mic. 6:8 may be fulfilled
and no one "go astray after . . . his own guilty inclination
to circumcise[3] in the Community the foreskin of the inclination and a stiff neck so as to establish a true foundation"
upon which Israel can be built into a community with which
God can make a covenant which will never be annulled. The
purpose of the establishment of this foundation is to
provide a means of atonement for the original members and
for those who join later to form a community and to act as
a judicial body to condemn those who transgress the precept.

---

[1] Cf. *ibid.*, cols. VII and VIII.

[2] A similar construction in CD 19:5f. expresses futurity.

[3] The awkwardness of the translation at this point attempts to reproduce
that of the original if Burrow's emendation is accepted. Clearly "to
circumcise" is subordinate, having no co-ordinating ו. It cannot be subordinate to "go astray after . . . his own guilty inclination", since the
two thoughts are incompatible. It must be subordinate to the fulfilment
of Mic. 6:8.

The arguments against Burrows' suggestion may now be
summarized.

i.   A radical emendation is involved and it is difficult
to see how the mistaken reading ‬ואאם could have arisen from
the highly intelligible אשם or האשמ. It is a bad principle
of textual criticism to resort to emendation when the text
as it stands can make some sense. Again, if one should prefer
the more difficult reading, ואאם is clearly preferable.

ii. The theological conceptions are not very clear, since
the Community would be atoning for itself.

iii. The sentence structure is awkward.

(c) A.M. Habermann[1] has suggested that the first letter of
ואאם be read as a *yod* and that a *kaph* should be supplied before it, giving כי אם. This suggestion has found wide acceptance.[2] It has the advantage of requiring less emendation than
that of Burrows. The adversative כי אם also follows on quite
well in the construction after "so that none shall walk in
the stubbornness of his heart" and serves at the same time
to bring the reader back to the series of infinitives which
had been temporarily abandoned.

The atonement doctrine involved would be the same as that
for Burrows' suggestion. It would also be open to the same
objections, except that the emendation is less radical and
the construction less awkward.

If Brownlee's suggestion is accepted, it is God that performs the atoning action, and he does this by establishing
a true foundation through changing people's hearts within the
Community.[3] Thus the means of atonement would be the same

---

[1] *Megilloth Midbar Yehuda*, Israel, 1959, p. 64.

[2] E.g. A. Dupont-Sommer, *The Essene Writings*, G. Lambert, *Le Manuel de Discipline du Désert de Juda*, Louvain, 1951; A.R.C. Leaney, *The Rule of Qumran and its Meaning*, London, 1966; Eduard Lohse, *op. cit.*; G. Vermes, *op. cit.*

[3] If one performs A for the purpose of accomplishing B, one performs B by means of A. The text tells us that the purpose of God's circumcising is to establish a true foundation for Israel and that in turn the purpose of this is to atone for present and future Community members. By saying that the ultimate purpose of changing men's hearts is to atone, he has

as we have seen already in 1QH 16:11 and f 2:13 and in 1QS
3:6-12:[1] a submissive spirit towards God. There is no mention of "spirit" in this connection, but the passage has affinities with 4:18-23, where a "spirit of holiness" is promised to purge the elect in the last days.

The passage is influenced by certain prophecies concerning
the last days after the return from exile. The language is
particularly reminiscent of Jer. 32:39-41, 50:5, Ezek. 16:60-
63. It also has affinities with CD 2:14-16, 3:2-4:4.

If the text is emended according to (b) or (c) above, the
members of the Community would be atoning for future members,
but the sense is certainly puzzling, since the latter are
divided into two classes in line 6 and these are naturally
interpreted as referring to the foundation members and those
who would join later respectively. Presumably atonement would
mean the provision of a means of grace through an atmosphere
of submission within the Community itself.

The mention of the judicial activity of the Community and
the condemnation of transgressors (6f.) does not indicate the
means of atonement, though it is related to it. These activities would be part of the means by which God would "circumcise in the Community the foreskin of the inclination."

C. 1QS 8:1-11

This passage is full of corrections in the manuscript.
There are also deliberate gaps, which some interpret as representing poetry.[2]

The preceding context may be briefly summarized. The attitude required of those who join is delineated, especially the
necessity of separating from the men of falsehood (5:7-20).
Those who enter are to be examined by the sons of Aaron according to their understanding and their deeds, and granted
rank accordingly. They are to be re-examined and re-graded

indicated that one of the means of atonement is changing hearts.

[1] Vid. supra, pp. 54-56.

[2] E.g. Brownlee, The Dead Sea Manual of Discipline, p. 32, n. 11.

annually (5:20-24). Directions are given for them to re-
buke one another in charity (5:25-6:1), and various rules
and penalties are prescribed (6:1-7:25).

The first part (lines 1-4) states that there must be twelve
men and three priests expert in everything the Law has to say
about certain matters which are listed by means of the familiar
ל plus the infinitive. It is better to take these as subordinate to "all that is revealed in the Torah" rather than
as expressing directly the function of the twelve men and
three priests, since what is being referred to by these infinitives is the content of the Old Testament, here loosely
called the Torah. The list quotes or alludes to the following
material.

Micah 6:8 (line 2),
the burden of the book of Deuteronomy ("faithfulness in the
land . . .", line 3),
Ps. 51:17 (line 3b),
Lev. 26:43 (line 3c),
apocalyptic material as interpreted by Qumran (line 4,
"according to the norm of time.").

It is important to see that, if the first sentence is construed in this way, no statement is made about any atoning
function for the twelve men and three priests. They have
simply to be perfectly versed in everything which the Scrip-
ture says about "accepting the punishment of iniquity amongst
those who execute justice[1] and accepting the refining trial
of adversity." It is, of course, unthinkable that their knowledge would be merely theoretical. They would have to be godly men, but it does not follow that they themselves have any
atoning function.[2] Now Lev. 26 states that when Israel is
exiled she will receive the punishment of her iniquity (רצה

---

[1] עשה משפט frequently has a judicial sense in the O.T., including in-
flicting punishment (e.g. Ps. 149:9). This sense fits here much better
than "live uprightly". For the punitive meaning elsewhere in the Scrolls
see 4QpNah. f 1/2:4.

[2] Their function would probably be to inform and inspire the decision-
making authorities, mentioned in 5:2f., whose duties involved the en-
forcement of the requirements of Mic. 6:8.

עֹון), and from the context it appears that this means not only suffering the punishment, but accepting it as justly deserved (Lev. 26:40f.). This was precisely the attitude which the Qumran community maintained. They took sides with God instead of with sinful mankind, even to the point of condemning themselves.

The Leviticus background helps us to understand the main thrust of lines 3f. In Lev. 26:43 Israel has to be punished because she refused God's judgements (מֹשְׁפֹּטִי), but the covenanters were to "execute judgement" (מֹשְׁפֹּט) on one another, submit to this and, as exiles in the desert, to endure adversity as prophesied in Lev. 26 and elsewhere.

The two remaining atonement references are closely parallel (lines 6 and 10). In both cases it is the land which is to be atoned for, the punishment of the wicked is mentioned immediately afterward, and God's approval of those who perform the atonement and the punishment is expressed by the term רֹצֹון "acceptance". Probably then the atonement is to be effected by the punishment of the wicked, so that the land will no longer be polluted with their abominations. Num. 35:33 is the basic Old Testament background for these phrases, for there the motifs of atoning for the land and punishing the wicked are linked in the same relationship as here.[1] Lev. 26 is full of concern for the land. Phinehas, too, performed an atoning function by punishing the wicked. He was one of the "true witnesses for judgement" (line 6), for as soon as he witnessed the sin, he acted in judgement.[2]

Brownlee and Wernberg-Møller have detected allusions here

---

[1] See too Deut. 32:43. Unlike these O.T. passages, however, the preposition governing "land" here is בֹּעֹד. This combination represents a usage not found in the O.T. which I have called the "Serek usage" (see my "Atonement Constructions", § 8), because it occurs characteristically in 1QS and 1QSa. The use of this preposition was probably intended to add a note of great solemnity, reflecting the "solemn Levitical" usage of the O.T. where בֹּעֹד governs the persons to be atoned for under special circumstances (*vid. infra*, pp. 126, 132).

[2] Num. 25:7. See 2Q21 (*Discoveries*, III, pp. 79f.) for truth and justice in a punitive context. According to CD 1:1, 2:2 the Community is to witness the justice of God's case against mankind on the grounds of what was revealed to them about God's dealings.

to the Servant passages in Isaiah.[1] These are undoubtedly
present, but it is highly questionable whether they point
to an atoning role for the Community. The phrase "elect of
good pleasure" (line 6) probably reflects Isa. 42:1, but it
does not follow that the later Servant Song,[2] which sets
forth an atoning function for the Servant, is also envisaged.
1QH 16:13 similarly echoes Isa. 42:1, but there the writer
has no atoning function for the elect one in view.

More significant are the sacrificial overtones in the use
of רצון. The acceptance by God which the sacrificial cultus
was designed to achieve is to be enjoyed by those who purify
the land by executing judgement. Saul had failed to do this
and was consequently rejected.[3] Phinehas had willingly performed it and it was "counted unto him for righteousness."[4]

D. 1QS 9:24

וכול הנעשה בו ירצה בנדבה, "and all that is done to him
(viz. to the Master of the Community, the Maskîl) he shall
accept willingly."

The preceding context of this sentence states that when the
Community is constituted in accordance with the principles
enunciated in 8:1-10 they are to withdraw into the desert
in fulfilment of Isa. 40:3, to "prepare the way of the Lord",
that is to study the Law (8:10-15). The earlier recension[5]
then goes on to outline the duties and spiritual qualities
of the Maskîl (9:11ff.). One of these is described in the
sentence under consideration, which is something of a *crux
interpretum*.

Brownlee and Wernberg-Møller take God to be the subject of
the "accept" in this clause. The former translates, "for

---

[1] *Vid.* Wernberg-Møller, *op. cit.*, p. 125, n. 16.

[2] Isa. 52:13-53:12. In 4QpNah. f 1/2:8 (*Discoveries*, V, p. 37) the
fragmentary phrase "the chosen ones of . . ." occurs in a context of
judgement, not salvation.

[3] I Sam. 15.

[4] Ps. 106:31.

[5] *Vid. supra*, p. 57 n. 1.

everything done by him, He will gladly accept", and the
latter, "Then everything which is done, by that he will be
accepted as a free will offering." Both these renderings
present the actions of the Master as some kind of sacrifice.
Nearly every word has ambiguities.

(a)   The first two words can be the subject, the object or
a *pendens* construction.

(b)   The third word can mean "by the Master", "to the Master",
"by God", or "by that" referring to a previous *pendens* construction.

(c)   The fourth word can be qal with the Master as the subject,
qal with God as the subject, niph'al with the Master as the
agent, or niph'al with God as the agent.

(d)   The last word can mean either "as a free-will offering"
or "willingly".

There are many possible combinations, but fortunately most
of them can be ruled out as ungrammatical or not making much
sense. The task of finding the most likely meaning is also
facilitated by the fact that some of the alternatives are in-
trinsically less likely than others.

(a)   The *pendens* construction is not very likely here. One
would expect rather ובכול. The clause is a short one and
unlikely to give rise to anacoluthon.

(b)   Since Hebrew idiom prefers direct expression rather than
passive constructions with the agent expressed, the meanings
"by the Master" or "by God" are less likely than the alternatives. עשה ב can mean "to do to" or "to perform *something*
against *someone*" in the Scrolls.[1]

(c)   The Master is more likely the subject of "accept" than
God, since the verb to accept, רצה is used again in the following line with reference to the Master and is so translated
by both Brownlee and Wernberg-Møller. Indeed, there seems to
be a loose parallelism which demands this sense in line 25;
but it is equally demanded by a similar parallelism in line
24, as well as by the whole context which is all about man's
acceptance of God's ways. The cognate רצון occurs in lines

---

[1] *Vid.*, 1QS 1:26, 5:12f., CD 1:2, 12; 8:11, 1QH 15:19, 1QpHab. 9:1-2.

23 and 24 in the sense of that which is acceptable to God,
but this is its normal sense in this scroll.

(d) בנדבה occurs elsewhere in the Scrolls only in 1QH 14:24,
where the text is too fragmentary to determine the meaning,
and in 1QH 15:10, where the meaning is simply "willingly"
and cannot be "by a free-will offering". The phrase also
occurs in the Old Testament in Num. 15:3 and Ps. 54:8. Both
these instances are classified under "free-will" rather than
"voluntary offering" by G. Lisowsky,[1] but the contexts are
sacrificial and the meaning "free-will offering" is quite
possible.

The following are the most likely translations of the
clause.

i.   everything which is done to him shall be accepted
      willingly,
ii.   everything which is done to him, he shall accept
      willingly,
iii. everything which is done by him shall be accepted
      as a free-will offering,
iv.   everything which is done by him God shall accept as
      a free-will offering.

i. and ii. do not involve any atonement sense. iii. and iv.
may have atonement significance, since the Master's actions
are described in sacrificial terms. iii. and iv. involve
interpretations of the individual terms which inherently
are less likely than those involved in i. and ii. The sacrificial interpretation also involves the introduction of a
new thought, foreign to the context. This passage concerns
man's acceptance of God's actions, not God's acceptance of
man's. The Master is to love and do God's will above every
thing else. Even his loves and hates are to be subject to
God (9:21). God's will means not only what God wills man
to do, but also what God wills to be done to man. The Master
is to delight in this too. He will take pleasure in God's
commandments (9:25), but also in God's activity both in nature
(9:26-10:10, 14f.), in His judgements against sin, including

---

[1] *Op. cit.*, p. 903.

that of the Master himself (10:11-13, 17, 23f.) and in His
salvation and forgiveness (10:14f., 17).

Although the sacrificial sense of these words cannot be
accepted as the most likely, meanings i. and ii. are linked
to a vital element in the Community's soteriology. Israel
is suffering for her sin. This suffering will continue until
there is repentance, which is to take the form of the acceptance of God's punishment and confession that it was justly
merited.[1] This attitude is to be adopted by the Community
as a first step towards the repentance of Israel as a whole.[2]
The Master of the Community is to display this attitude in
an exemplary manner as expressed in the concluding hymn,[3] for
unless he manifested this spirit himself, he could not be
relied on to insist on it in the postulants and members whom
it was his duty to assess.[4]

E. 1QS 2:8 AND GOD AS THE SUBJECT OF THE ATONING ACTION

ולוא יסלח לכפר עווניך

4QSb reads עוונכה as the last word here.[5] This confirms
Wernberg-Møller's suggestion that the "singular is probably
intended in our passage", the 1QS reading representing a
variant spelling.[6]

It is uncertain whether the atonement is the means or the

---

[1] Lev. 26:40-42.

[2] 1QSa 1:1-3. 1QM 1:1-2:9 presupposes that in the last days Israel will
be converted in large enough numbers for the Community to be in control
of the Temple.

[3] 10:5-end.

[4] 9:12-19. Carmignac notes that this is a citation of Ecclus. 2:4.
He translates "tout ce qui lui arrive il agréera volontiers". Vid.
Les textes de Qumran, Paris, 1961, pp. 66f. Some Greek texts of Sirach,
together with the Syro-Hexapla, read in Ecclus. 2:4 "accept readily whatsoever is brought upon you." Vid. R.H. Charles, Apocrypha and Pseudepigrapha of the Old Testament, Vol. I, London, 1913, p. 322. Unfortunately this passage is lacking in extant Hebrew texts of Sirach. LXX word
order corresponds with that of 1QS 9:24.

[5] Milik, Rev. Bib., 67 (1960), p. 412.

[6] Op. cit., p. 53, n. 23.

result of forgiveness. Wernberg-Møller[1] has pointed to the
combination of סלח and כפר in Lev. 4:26, 31, "and the priest
shall make atonement for him from his sin and it shall be
forgiven him." There the atonement is clearly a means of
forgiveness, so perhaps the two verbs should be considered
to be in the same relation here. We may translate, "and may
he not forgive by atoning for your iniquity."

Clearly כפר would then mean more than "pardon" or "forgive",
for it would signify some means or grounds of forgiveness.
It is possible that the writer has atonement rituals in mind
and that what he is expressing is the prayer that God may not
accept the sacrifices of the wicked. This would accord readily with the sentiments expressed later in 2:15-3:12, but this
hypothesis cannot be accepted until a possible objection has
been faced.

It is probable that here God is to be understood as the
subject of the atoning action.[2] Now in the Old Testament
God is never said to atone for those sins for which expiatory
provision is made in the cultus.[3] How then can לכפר here refer
to sacrificial cultus, if God is the subject of the atoning
action? The fact that this is not stated to have taken place,
but is deplored as undesirable, mitigates the difficulty some-

---

[1] *Ibid.*

[2] Similarly 1QS 11:14, CD 2:5, 3:18, 4:6f., 9, 10, 20:34, 1QH 4:37, 17:12.

[3] Deut. 21:8 is no exception, since the slaying of the heifer was not
properly even a sacrifice, still less an expiation, for no expiation could
be made for innocent blood except by the death of the murderer (Num. 35:31-
33). It is rather a solemn declaration, as if the elders were saying, "If
we are not speaking the truth, may we become like this heifer." It is
also probable that the covenant sacrifices, like that described in Jer.
34:8-19, had something of this character (cf. I Sam. 11:7 and see Leon
Morris, *The Apostolic Preaching of the Cross*, London, 1955, pp. 63f.).

II Chron. 30:18 is conceivably another exception, but the situation
there is presented as being highly irregular. There seems to have been
no Levitical provision for atonement for one who had eaten the passover
knowing himself to be unclean. If one were unclean at the normal time of
eating, one could delay for a month. These Israelites from the northern
kingdom had already delayed because of the general atmosphere of neglect
and were still unclean at the second month. All the king could do was to
implore God's mercy on their behalf. Presumably it would have been an
even greater sin not to have kept the feast (Num. 9:1-13).

what. It is possible that the writer is well aware that
cultic atonement cannot avail for those guilty of the "deeds
of darkness" (line 7) that are characteristic of the men of
Belial's lot. He would then be saying something like this:
"Your sins are such that there is no provision in the cult
for their expiation. If, in spite of this, you offer sacrifices and try to bribe God, may he have no regard for them!"
To see whether this interpretation can be accepted as it is,
or needs to be modified, we should bear in mind the Old
Testament usage of כפר.[1] The Old Testament had already used
sacrificial terms to describe right attitudes and actions
before God,[2] but only once expiatiory terms.[3] 1QS is more
ready than the Old Testament to use expiatory terms in this
connection. Atonement is effected in 3:6-11 "by an upright
and humble spirit" and in 5:6 by the circumcision "in the
Community of the foreskin of the inclination". Are these,
then, a כפור, something offered to God as a substitute[4] for
the obedience which is lacking in the rest of Israel? The
substitutionary aspect of atonement seems to be absent from
the thinking of 1QS. It is rather solidarity thinking that
underlies the concept of the atoning efficacy of the Community's righteousness. The Members were to be a foundation
of holiness and truth for Israel.[5] Clearly the atonement
works by the Community's becoming a means of grace for those
who join it.[6]

Alongside of this, another means of atonement is elaborated:
the punishment of the guilty. This had its roots in the Old
Testament.[7] The Community often thought of its atoning func-

---

[1] Vid. infra, pp. 124ff.

[2] Ps. 4:5, 51:17, Hos. 14:2.

[3] Prov. 16:6, where the construction is "Isaianic" (vid. supra, p. 55
n. 1), as it is also here.

[4] Cf. Num. 8:16-19, where the Levites are said "to make atonement for the
children of Israel" by serving in the tabernacle as substitutes for the
first-born.

[5] 5:5.

[6] 5:7, unless Brownlee's theory be accepted (vid. supra, pp. 61-64),
when probably God would forgive them directly.

[7] Num. 25:13, 35:33, Deut. 32:43, Isa. 43:3.

tion in close connection with its judging activity.[1] This
is especially the case where the object of the atonement is
the land.[2] Here, too, solidarity thinking forms the basis.
The whole of Israel would suffer as long as evil was being
tolerated in her midst.

One may distinguish three aspects of the imagery inherent
in the use of כפר and cognates to describe the process of
reconciliation with God: substitution, gift, propitiation
(turning away wrath). In 1QS the substitutionary aspect is
eclipsed, the gift aspect emerges as a metaphor for the Community's obedience and discipline, including its judgement
of the wicked, and the propitiatory aspect remains intact
and is to be seen even in this passage. A prayer against
atonement is a prayer for wrath.[3]

F. 1QS 11:13-15 AND THE RIGHTEOUSNESS OF GOD IN ATONEMENT

After the description of the duties and qualities of the
Master (9:12-26), there follows a hymn for his use, described
as the "heave-offering of the lips"[4] and consisting of praise
to God, including a doxology of judgement.[5]

The Master is to praise God at the appointed seasons

---

[1] 1QS 5:6f., 8:6f., 10. See too 1Q 34 1:5f. (*Discoveries*, I, p. 153).

[2] 8:3, 6, 10.

[3] 2:9. The intercessors, also mentioned in this line, are probably
angels. Cf. Job 33:24, I Enoch 15:1ff.

[4] It is almost universally agreed that הרומה should be supplied in the
gap before שפתים: Brownlee, Dupont-Sommer, Habermann, Lambert, Lohse,
Vermes, Wernberg-Møller. This would tend to confirm the interpretation
suggested below (p. 83) for the phrase "heave offering of the lips for
judgement" in 9:4f., since this hymn is in fact largely a doxology of
judgement. In 10:8 he actually says that the engraved precept shall be
on his tongue "as a fruit of praise, the portion of my lips", whilst
10:11 tells us the Master's transgressions would be before him as "an
engraved precept". Thus praise, the precept and the speaker's guilt
are linked in a doxology of judgement and the Master praises God not
only in hymns like this, but also in his teaching and judging in the
Community.

[5] *Vid infra*, p. 83, n. 2.

according to the movements of the heavenly bodies (10:1-8).[1]
Praise should be given for God's commandments and in accordance with God's commandments. Indeed, to speak of God's
commandments is to praise him (10:8-10). God's judgements
of the Master are righteous, for God is his righteousness
(צדקי), goodness and holiness. He will accept God's judgements upon him as well as God's teaching for him (10:10-13).[2]
In all his daily activities he will praise God (10:13-15).
Even when he is in distress he will give thanks, for God
judges all, and everything He does is truth. He will praise
God for His salvation too (10:15-17). He will not be envious
of the wicked in their prosperity, but await with patience,
yet longingly, the time of their judgement (10:17-20). For
those who repent he will not retain his wrath, but he will
show no compassion to the backsliders until their way is perfect (עד תום דרכם). Belial, folly and deceit he will eschew
(10:21-23). He will declare the righteous acts (צדקות)[3] of
God and the treachery of man, until his punishment is complete (10:23f.).[4] He will dispense knowledge with discretion

---

[1] Behind this concern for praying at the right time lies the sentiment,
common in the inter-testamental literature, that since the heavenly
bodies obey God so exactly and perfectly, man should do the same. See
Samuel Iwry, "A New Designation for the Luminaries in Ben Sira and in
the Manual of Discipline (1QS)," *BASOR*, 200 (Dec., 1970), p. 41, and cf.
1QH 12:4-11, I Enoch 2:1-5:5; 21; 41:7ff.

[2] In the O.T. צדק is the most general word for righteousness, whereas
צדקה signifies God's saving righteousness. Here too צדק is clearly
linked with God's punishment, but it is accepted by the Master and made
an object of praise. This is an example of that accepting of punishment
(רצה עוון) which Lev. 26:40-42 declares to be the prelude to God's blessing Israel again. צדק is linked closely with God's goodness here. Does
the author conceive God's צדק to be the source of His צדקה?

[3] If both the righteous acts of God and the treachery of man are connected with the punishment mentioned here (see also next note), צדקה
admits of a punitive flavour, contrary to O.T. usage, but not to that of
the Scrolls. Cf. *supra*, p. 9 n. 3, 43 n. 1.

[4] עד תום פשעם. Wernberg-Møller translates, "to the point of his complete
sinfulness." In the light of the very similar expression in line 21,
however, "until their way is perfect", it is very probable that עד has
a temporal reference and should be translated "until". Furthermore, it
is possible to find clues to the meaning in similar expressions from
previous literature. Brownlee translates, "until their transgression is
ended" or "until their transgression is complete" and adduces Dan. 8:23
and Gen. 15:14. In both these passages there is the image of transgression
as a liquid filling up a cup of wrath. It is when the cup is full that it

and seek to maintain faithfulness and judgement (משפט) like
a strong wall of defense for God's saving righteousness (צדקה
10:24f.).[1] The Master will be patient with the erring members

---

will have to be drunk by the sinners. The former passage has cognates of
the two words for transgression, but it is the closest verbal parallel
mentioned by Brownlee. He also refers to Lam. 4:22 and Dan. 9:24 as
suggesting a different interpretation from the one he has adopted. In the
former it is the "iniquity" of Israel that is complete. This is a recognized term for punishment too (e.g. Lev. 26:43, Isa. 40:2) and is usually
so translated here (RV, RSV, NEB). Dan. 9:24 is in the rather obscure
passage about the seventy weeks, but it is quite feasible that this
verse refers to the suffering of punishment due to transgression, so
that all Jacob's troubles may come to an end.

The present writer has been led to translate the phrase as "until the
punishment for their transgression is complete" after consideration of
Lam. 4:22 and Dan. 9:24, but especially of a certain sentence in I Enoch
22. In that chapter Enoch is given a vision of four hollow places of
waiting for the souls of the departed:-

i.   for the righteous,
ii. for sinners who have not been punished in life,
iii. for the righteous who have been killed by sinners and who make
     accusation,
iv. "for the spirits of men who are not righteous but sinners, who were
     complete in transgression," (R.H. Charles, *op. cit.* II, p. 203).
     These spirits will not be slain, but they will not be raised either.

Clearly there are two groups of righteous and two of sinners. Of the
righteous, one group has suffered in this life more than was due to them,
and of the sinners, one group has suffered less than was due to them.
What is more natural than to suppose that the other groups of each class,
i. and iv., have already suffered what is due? One would then say that
the fourth place was "for the spirits of men who were not righteous but
sinners, the punishment for whose transgression was complete." Their fate
would appear more equitable, since it would probably seem wrong to the
author that people who were completely sinful, "complete in transgression",
should be spared the second death, which in any case is never explicitly
stated in I Enoch to involve eternal punishment for human beings. This
gives the closest parallel known to the present writer for 1QS 11:24, and
each passage illuminates the other. Both involve translating פשע by
"punishment for transgression", but this should cause no difficulty, since
it is quite usual for Hebrew words for sin to bear the meaning of "consequence of sin" too. פשע is no exception (see Job 14:17, Ps. 39:8, 103:
12, Isa. 24:20).

[1] Literally: "to maintain faithfulness and a strong judgement for the
righteousness of God." Brownlee has pointed to Isa. 24:2 in connection
with this passage. There are many linguistic echoes of Isa. 24:1-3 here.
Isa. 24 speaks of a strong fenced city into which the righteous and faithful nation is to enter. In 1QS this fence is the secrecy surrounding the
Community's knowledge and also its practice of משפט. Behind this pro-
tective wall the saving righteousness of God will be able to operate.
Indeed the wall itself is God's saving righteousness, for God saves
through the Community and its discipline. Thus God's משפט is a necessary
part of his צדקה.

of the Community and reply humbly even to the haughty (10:26-
11:2). His justification comes from God, who will wipe out
his transgressions by His righteous acts (בצדקות). He knows
this because he has been privileged to gaze on God's marvellous deeds and to receive his light from the fountain of
God's knowledge and his justification (משפטי) from the source
of His righteousness (צדקותו).[1] The vision of all this has
been hidden from everyone but the elect who share God's counsel along with the angels and as a Community constitute a
foundation for eternal holiness (11:2-9). As a member of
wicked humanity the Master confesses that he can do no good
except by God's grace (11:9-11). Even if he stumbles, God
will restore him. His justification is through the righteousness (משפטי בצדקה אל) of God who will set him on the right
path again (11:9-13).

There follows the passage under consideration, where the
concept of atonement is introduced. Before discussing the
precise meaning of this atonement, something should be said
about the interpretation of משפט in this section. The central
idea is of judgement, but the image is of a king acting as
judge. His judgements are equivalent to law and we have the
word used in this sense in 9:25, 10:7, 9. If God's judgements
are adverse, condemnation results and the word is almost equivalent to "punishment". This sense appears in 10:11, 20, 25.
If God's judgement is favourable, there is acquittal or justification. This sense seems to fit best in all the occurrences
in column 11 (lines 2, 5, 10, 12, 14). Some scholars translate the word as "judgement" even here,[2] but 11:9-11 makes
it clear that the Master felt himself in need of something

---

[1] Wernberg-Møller reads משפטו in line 5 and takes it in apposition to
וצדקותו, translating: "From the fountain of His righteousness, His justice,
the light has come into my heart from His wonderful mysteries." He believes משפטו to be a gloss which has crept into the text. Whatever reading is followed or interpretation adopted, משפט is closely connected with
צדקה at some stage in the Community's history. Either the former comes
from the latter, or the two are the same thing. If the former comes from
the latter, it means "justification" and the latter can mean "saving
righteousness", but if the two are identical, צדקה would have a wider
meaning and be almost equivalent to צדק.

[2] E.g. Leaney, Wernberg-Møller. Carmignac (*Les Textes de Qumran, ad loc.*)
has "jugement, droit."

like a justification in the Pauline sense. It is not simply
the case of a righteous person waiting to be vindicated.[1]
An element of ambiguity arises because of the Master's acceptance of all God's judgements, in every sense of the word
outlined above. His attitude, therefore, gives no clue as to
whether it is justification or punishment which he is accepting willingly.[2] Since God is the king of the universe, his
judgements include all his decisions concerning man. Among
these are his decrees of election. Perhaps it is in this way
that the justifying judgement can be also a reforming one
(11:10b, 12).

Atonement in this passage is most clearly linked with God's
goodness, but the context provides a link with his righteousness too. This righteousness (צדקה) is said to bring the
speaker's judgement and also his purification. The imagery
of the passage belongs to the court of a king. A member of
a guilty race has been "drawn near". Sentence has been pronounced upon him (משפטי, 14), but he accepts this as a just
and true judgement, so much so that he can speak of it in
parallel with the mercy which has drawn him near (13f.). The
changes of tense place the situation shortly after the speaker's reception at court. His sentence is already a thing of
the past and the favour which the king has displayed towards
him in receiving him gives him confidence that he will always
forgive and purify him. Probably this purification (טהר)
implies reformation.[3] As for the forgiveness, the use of
כפר here implies that the king has put away his wrath.[4]

Certain of the themes used are found in Hos. 2:19: חסד,
צדק, משפט and רחמים, but there the image is of a betrothal,

---

[1] Cf. Lyonnet, "Justification, jugement, rédemption, principalement dans
l'Epître aux Romains," *Littérature et théologie pauliniennes*, Bruges,
1960, pp. 174f.

[2] Furthermore, God's punitive judgements are probably seen as a means of
his justification, because it is by these that he is purified. This adds
to the ambiguity in the use of משפט. Even its saving effect is not necessarily an indication that it means "justification" *tout court*.

[3] The same word is used in 4:21 to describe the practical effects of a
holy spirit within a man.

[4] *Vid. supra*, p. 73.

not a royal pardon. Nevertheless, the writer probably had
the Hosea passage in mind as expressing the future acceptance
of Israel in spite of her unworthiness.

This theme of unworthiness is re-inforced by the use of the
preposition בעד after כפר. Wernberg-Møller[1] directs his
readers at this point to CD 3:18 and C. Rabin's note thereon.
Rabin remarked that this preposition only occurs after כפר
in Exod. 32:30.[2] This statement will need some qualification,
since כפר בעד is also to be found in Lev. 9:7 *bis*, 16:6, 11,
17, 24, Ezek. 45:17 and II Chron. 30:18. One should say rather that only in Exod. 32:30 is this preposition used after
כפר to signify the sin to be atoned for, as it is in 1QS 11:
14. The Exodus passage should not be given exclusive consideration as the background here, for in Exodus it is not
God who is to atone, but Moses. The verse in II Chronicles
should also be given due weight, for God is the subject of
the atoning action as he is here, although there persons,
not sins are spoken of as the object. These two constitute
the immediate Old Testament background for כפר בעד here, but
it is significant that this phrase dominates in the description
tion of the Day of Atonement rituals in Lev. 16 in contrast
to כפר על, which is the favourite term for ritual atonement
in the rest of the priestly writings, but is extremely rare
in these scrolls. Perhaps these priests in the Judæan desert,
long barred from the Temple services, found little to interest
them in the Old Testament passages about ritual atonement, except those concerning the Day of Atonement ceremony.[3] Exod.
32:30 and II Chron. 30:18 both concern a general apostasy of
Israel. This was likewise the situation at the birth of the
Qumran Community, and it is natural that they should meditate
on these passages when they thought of atonement for Israel,
rather than on those sections of the Pentateuch which pre-

---

[1] *Op. cit.*, p. 153, n. 39.

[2] *The Zadokite Documents*, ed. and tr. by Chaim Rabin, Oxford, 1954,
ad loc.

[3] Even 1QM 2:5 has בעד. For the importance of the Day of Atonement in
the Community's calendar see 1QpHab 11:6f.

scribe rituals for more normal circumstances.[1]

How are God's righteousness and his atoning activity linked
in 1QS 11:13-15? Both God's צדקה and his חסד are stated to
be the source of the speaker's justification. His atonement
is ascribed to God's goodness but the thought is extremely
close to that of his saving justice and his mercy, or kindness
חסד. Furthermore, the purpose of all this saving action is
that he might "confess to God His justice" or "praise God for
His justice צדק." The writer did not use this word without
any regard for the fact that it is a cognate of צדקה. Surely,
then, man has seen God's צדק through his צדקה. Now to confess
God's צדק is to utter a doxology of judgement. According to
Lev. 26:40-42 the confession of God's justice even in his
punishments was to be the preliminary to Israel's restoration.
The whole life of the Qumran Community was such a confession
on behalf of Israel. They acknowledged God's justice and were
willing to accept his judgements against them. In so doing
they found a judgement of God which was for them (justification) and the assurance that God had accepted them, drawing
them near to share his counsel, and that he would pardon their
iniquities and cleanse them from all sin. This adds another
dimension to their praise of God's character as righteous
(צדק). Not only do they accept all his decisions that flow
from this character (משפט), but they have also learned to
appreciate his activity in pardoning and purifying them, thus
achieving practically a state of righteousness in their midst
(צדקה).[2]

It is to be noted that the Old Testament passages which
provide the background to much of the vocabulary here (Exod.
32:30, Lev. 16, II Chron. 30:18, Hos. 2:19) have to do with
Israel's national acceptance by God. In this connection it
is significant that the Master of the Community sings this
hymn as the leader of the group which in turn is to be the
foundation stone for the renewed and sanctified Israel that

---

[1] See 1QH 17:12 (*supra*, p. 50 n. 1), where the same usage occurs.

[2] In this they were following in the footsteps of their Founder (1QH
9:9-23; *supra*, pp. 29f.).

is to come.

The rest of the hymn may be briefly summarized. He now
embarks upon the praise of God's righteousness, for it was
in view of this that God had manifested his favour towards
him (line 15). He prays that God may establish his deeds
in righteousness (צדק) even as it pleases Him to do for the
elect. Without God man can do no good at all. What is man
before the Almighty (11:15-e)?

G. ATONEMENT IN THE CONTEXT OF 1QS SOTERIOLOGY

The idea of salvation finds a cosmic setting in 1QS due to
the doctrine of the two spirits. Its culmination is to be
the enjoyment of "all the glory of Adam" by those whose way
of life is perfect. The Community is to provide the context
for such a way of life. This cosmic dimension, however, in
no way constitutes a shift of emphasis from Israel as the
object of God's saving designs. The Community is to function
as an authentic basis for Israel, so that by joining it she
may be saved.

There must be utter whole-heartedness on the part of those
who join, involving the espousal of God's attitude towards
everything, and acceptance of all his judgements both favourable and adverse, separation from outsiders and submission
to the Community's discipline. Salvation is mediated by life
in the Community and the attitude or spirit of submission
which is manifested there is spoken of in terms of an atonement. Here the gift aspect of כפר emerges as a metaphor.
There may be overtones of the gift metaphor too in connection
with the other means of atonement mentioned in this document:
the punitive activity of the Members.[1]

Atonement continues to imply an end of God's wrath and a
full acceptance of the sinner. Its real basis is God's goodness alone. Far from the Community regarding itself in a

---

[1] *Supra*, p. 67. This Phinehas-type atonement is for the land, not for
people as such. It is related to Num. 35:33 and the exilic theme of the
desolation of the land elaborated in Lev. 26:31-35, 43 and in Dan. 8:13,
27, 9:18, 26f., 11:31, 12:11 (root שמם).

Suffering Servant role in 1QS, the underlying assumption is
that the bearing of another's iniquity is to be avoided (נשא
עוון, 5:14f., 6:1). What is enjoined upon the Members is
rather the acceptance of the punishment of their own iniquity
(רצה עוון, 8:3), in fulfilment of the requirement of Lev.
26:41f. There is no hint that they were doing this vicarious-
ly, though it was to have a saving effect upon the rest of
Israel by constituting a foundation upon which future penitents could be built. These penitents, of course, would have
to accept their own punishment as an essential ingredient in
their repentance.

CHAPTER IV:

ATONEMENT DURING THE HASMONÆAN PERIOD AND IN CD

A.   THE ADDITION TO THE MANUAL OF DISCIPLINE

The material considered so far is dated by Starcky within the Maccabæan period.[1] We now turn to the documents he assigns to the period immediately preceding the earthquake, which in 31 B.C. destroyed the Community centre at Qumran.[2] 1QS 8:15b-9:11, 1QSa, 1QSb, 4Q Test. and CD. Starcky dates the first three of these in the Hasmonæan period and CD in the Pompeian.

The section which has been inserted into the Manual of Discipline follows the passage (1QS 8:10-15) which states that when the Community is constituted in accordance with the principles enunciated in 8:1-10, the members are to withdraw into the desert in fulfilment of Isa. 40:3. The "way of the LORD" mentioned in this prophecy is the study of the Law and the prophets (8:13-16). The new section continues with a passage in which three kinds of sins are envisaged (8:20-9:2):-

(a)   sins with a high hand,

(b)   sins with a slack hand,

(c)   inadvertent sins.

Both (a) and (b) are punished by expulsion. (b) seems to mean sins committed through carelessness due to lack of zeal. The atonement spoken of in the passage which follows (9:3-6) is best interpreted in connection with this exercise of the Community's discipline. The passage states more clearly than those studied so far that the Community has an atoning role,

---

[1] *Rev. Bib.*, 70 (1963), pp. 482f. Starcky believes that the whole of 1QH and of the earliest recension of 1QS are the work of the Founder. According to the view taken in the present study, the whole of this could have been written in the Maccabæan period, though the Leader hymns of 1QH must have been written after the time of the Founder.

[2] *Vid. supra*, p. 5.

but the atonement is still for the land, not the wicked.
The phrase, "atone for the guilt of rebellion and the perverseness of sin" (9:4) falls short of a statement that the
wicked are being atoned for. This passage would seem to indicate that the wicked are to be judged (משפט, line 5) rather
than atoned for.

There is some uncertainty in the text in line 4, but whatever reading is followed the atonement is achieved without
the literal offering of sacrifice by means of the "offering
of the lips למשפט." This last phrase is interpreted by
Leaney, Lohse, Vermes and Wernberg-Møller as referring to
the rightness of the praise offered, whilst Brownlee and
Lambert translate it as expressing the fact that prayer is
counted as a sweet savour. It seems strange that this word,
which is so prominent in the Community's theology, should be
used in such a weak sense as these renderings suggest. Wherever the phrase למשפט occurs elsewhere in this scroll, it
refers to punishment or the discipline of the Community (5:12,
6:9, 8:6). It seems best to translate the phrase here in the
light of its meaning elsewhere in the scroll.[1] The Old Testament theme of sacrifices of praise is re-interpreted here
in terms of the discipline of the Community. Not only is the
judgement of the sinner well-pleasing to God (cf. 8:6f., 10),
but the sinner's judgement upon himself, whereby he confesses
his sins, also gives glory to God and of itself constitutes
a sacrifice. In this way confession is a kind of praise;
indeed, the same word is used for both in Hebrew.[2]

Temple imagery is prominent in this passage.[3] Atonement is
required in connection with the Temple so that men may ap-

---

[1] Vid. supra, pp. 73f.

[2] ידה and cognates. See Von Rad, op. cit., I, p. 357. This word is
found in the Old Testament in connection with what Von Rad has called
"doxologies of judgement", where the sinner confesses his guilt and
declares that God is righteous (Lev. 26:20, Josh. 7:19, I Kings 8:33,
Ezra 10:11).

[3] B. Gärtner has shown that an important key to the self-understanding
of the Qumran covenanters is the fact that they thought of themselves
as the true Temple of God (Temple and Community in Qumran and the New
Testament, Cambridge, 1965).

proach the holiness of God. According to line 6 this is to
be achieved through the sons of Aaron fulfilling once again
their true function in the midst of the יחד, the ideal unity
of Israel as a worshipping covenant community before God in
the last days.[1] The Community itself is the Temple and its
activity is the sacrifice. This activity is both verbal and
practical. The verbal activity, called here "the offering
of the lips in the exercise of judgement", includes the solemn
ceremonies of covenant renewal with their blessings and curs-
ings, the judgement on the conduct of Members, confession of
sin and praise to God. The practical activity is described
simply as "perfection of way". Thus evil is judged, both in
oneself and in others, and thereby God is praised, for it is
God's judgement of evil which is accepted in this way. Evil
is also judged practically, in oneself by repentance and a
perfect way of life and in others by the discipline of the
Community and ultimately by the holy war. In these too God is
glorified. There is no hint that this activity of judgement
and perfection is thought to be a work of supererogation,
producing a surplus of merit which can be transferred to the
wicked. There is no atonement for the wicked but only for the
land. If God is to have mercy on the land and deliver it from
gentile pollution, then he must see Israel obeying the Law.[2]
The Community is the beginning of this, "a foundation of the

---

[1]   In the O.T. יחד means simply "together". The choice of this word by
Qumran to designate itself may have been influenced by its use in the
Pentateuch for the tribes of Israel united under the covenant and the Law
(Exod. 19:8, Deut. 33:5), in the Psalms for Israel united in the cult
before Yahweh (Ps. 34:3, 102:22, 122:3, 133:1) and in the prophets for
the tribes re-united in the land in the last days (Isa. 52:8f., Hos. 1:11,
Mic. 2:12). *Vid. supra*, p. 13 n. 3.

[2]   The use of כפר with the preposition על governing the sin to be forgiven
probably indicates concern about gentile pollution. In the O.T. this construction is found in Jer. 18:23 and Ps. 79:9. In the former, Jeremiah
asks God not to pardon his enemies. The latter is more likely to be the
background of the present passage. Ps. 79 opens with the complaint that
Jerusalem has been defiled and devastated by the heathen and begs God to
punish the gentiles and forgive Israel. See too *supra*, p. 80 n. 1.
The same construction occurs in Lev. 4:35, 5:13, 18 in cultic contexts.
If this is also in the background, it indicates that כפר is being used
metaphorically here, as part of the temple imagery.

spirit of holiness for eternal truth",[1] so that Israelites as
they join the Community may become a holy temple to the Lord.
The whole concept is based on corporate thinking. It is "for
Israel", that is, "for those who walk in perfection" (line 6),
because those Israelites who do not walk in perfection simply
do not count as Israel. There can be no atonement for the
land unless God can see at least some Israelites who are
pleasing to him, and the Qumran covenanters were attempting
to make at least a start in this direction in spite of the
prevailing apostasy.

B. THE MESSIANIC RULE (1QSa)

This title, which has been given by Vermes to the annexe
to the Manual of Discipline (1QSa),[2] emphasises the important
fact that this document was not intended to be a rule for the
Qumran community as such, but for the whole of Israel in the
last days, when the masses would repent and become integrated
with the Community. This conversion would precede the final
war against the forces of evil (1:26).

Only the opening lines are important for atonement doctrine
(1:1-3). These state that the Community has separated itself
from the majority of Israelites and from the surrounding evil
so as to atone for the land.[3] The context of this atonement
saying seems to indicate that the *modus operandi* is the survival of a faithful remnant, affording an opportunity for the
rest of Israel to join it when God's time of salvation comes.
Atonement is for the land and it is effected by the repentance

---

[1] Line 3. The construction which immediately follows, לכפר with no ו
preceding, indicates that this "foundation of the spirit of holiness" is
a means of atonement. The ideas involved are almost identical with those
of 5:5ff., but here the right attitude within the Community, which is the
ultimate ground of atonement, is called "the spirit of holiness".

Cf. Brownlee's mature assessment of the significance of Qumran atonement: "The idea would seem to be that the piety of a few enables God to
look with favor upon the Holy Land". *Meaning of the Qumran Scrolls for
the Bible*, p. 149.

[2] Vermes, *op. cit.*, p. 118.

[3] בעד. It is the "Serek usage" again. *Vid. supra*, p. 66 n. 1.

of the masses. Only then can the land be cleansed from
gentile pollution through the mobilization of the nation
under the messianic figures who will emerge at that time.[1]

C. THE BOOK OF BLESSINGS (1QSb)

This document contains a series of blessings to be pronounced in the last days upon the faithful, the High Priest,
the priests and the Messiah of Israel. The following points
are worthy of note.

(a)   Great prominence is accorded to the High Priest and to
      the priests.
(b)   The main function of the priests is to teach.
(c)   A sacrificial function is mentioned for the High Priests
      only.
(d)   Cultic sacrifice is considered to be pleasing to God
      and is spoken of as affecting God's attitude to the
      worshippers (3:1-3).

Clearly the idea of cultic atonement remains quite compatible
with the Qumran expectations for the last days.

D. 4Q TESTIMONIA

This document consists of quotations from Deut. 5:28f.,
18:18f., Num. 24:15-17, Deut. 33:8-11, Josh. 6:26 and an
Essene work called the *Psalms of Joshua*. It is a collection
of brief texts about the last days. The first three sections
present what is probably intended to be taken as prophecies
concerning the eschatological prophet, the Messiah of Israel
and the Messiah of Aaron. Each section ends with the threat
of divine judgement. These three "Messianic" sections are
all taken from the Torah. The section which follows them
applies the curse on Jericho to the city of Jerusalem and
reproaches the enemies of Qumran for having rebuilt Jerusalem
amidst ungodliness.

---

[1]   The stress on the Promised Land is present even in the description of
the Messianic banquet with which the document closes (2:11-22), for the
word used for "wine" (תירוש) means wine as an agricultural product.

In a document of this character not every detail is important as an indication of the Community's thought, since
many phrases are included merely as part of the quotation.
The general character of the quotations chosen, however, is
very significant and the stress on judgement is the dominant
note alongside of the Messianic motif. Keeping God's word
and covenant for the Levites involved them in destroying
apostate Israelites after the worship of the golden calf
(lines 15-17). The Qumran covenanters considered themselves
to be under the same obligation (1QS 9:21-23, 1QM 1:2f.).

E. ATONEMENT IN THE CONTEXT OF THE SOTERIOLOGY OF CD

The Damascus Document takes the form of an ancient covenant between a sovereign and his vassals. It starts by re-
counting the saving acts of the King (God) and then describes
the behaviour expected of his faithful subjects (the Qumran
covenanters). The first part of the work has been called by
Rabin "the Admonition" (ms. A, pages I-VIII, ms. B)[1] and the
second part "the Laws" (ms. A, pages IX-XVI). Rabin has per-
ceived that the first part is a mosaic of quotations.[2] Because of this it is sometimes difficult to know whether to
understand a phrase as part of a biblical allusion or as
referring to some event in the history of the Community.[3]

The aim of the work is to bring into the covenant those who
wish to join or renew their association. The first part explains the desirability of the covenant, showing how the out-
come of Israel's past relations with God was such that there
was no salvation for any outside of this covenant.[4] Only in
this way could genuine adherence to God's commandments be
practised. Outside of this was the threat of "great flaming

---

[1] The two pages of ms. B will be referred to in this essay as "19" and
"20" respectively.

[2] *The Zadokite Documents*, ix, but this is the <u>means</u> of presenting something and one of the things being presented could be parts of the history
of the Community, *pace* Rabin, *ibid*: "not a history of the sect."

[3] Cf. *infra*, p. 94, n. 1.

[4] For a discussion of the identity of this covenant see Jaubert, *La
notion d'alliance*, pp. 219-222.

wrath" (2:5f.), inside, everlasting life and all the glory
of Adam (3:20).

The work opens with the theme of God's litigation (ריב)
against sinful mankind and especially Israel,[1] in which God is
both prosecutor and judge, and those who "know righteousness"
(צדק) are witnesses to the justice of the whole proceedings
(1:1-2).

When Israel forsook (עזב) God,[2] he forsook them in his
wrath, but because of the covenant with the patriarchs[3] he
maintained a remnant from amongst them. 390 years after the
beginning of the age of wrath[4] he visited them and caused a
plant to grow in the soil:[5] a group of people who recognized
their own sinfulness (1:3-9). These sought the knowledge of
God for twenty years and were like blind men groping their
way, until, in response to their sincerity of heart, God
sent to them a Teacher of Righteousness to show them His
will both for their own conduct and for events to come in
this the last generation (1:9-12). The rest of Israel had

---

[1] An O.T. prophetic motif, e.g. Isa. 1:2ff., Mic. 1:2ff.

[2] Cf. II Chron. 15:2, 24:20, Isa. 54:7f. Rabin, *Zadokite Documents*,
p. 2, *ad* 1:3, n. 1) argues from the LXX that there is an allusion here
to Lev. 26:40.

[3] R. Le Déaut, "Une citation de Lévitique 26, 45 dans le *Document de
Damas* I, 4; VI, 2," *Rev. Qum.*, 6 (1967/8), points out that the Hebrew
phrase used here is known elsewhere only in CD 6:2 and in Lev. 26:45.
The allusion was first noticed by the original editor of CD, Solomon
Schechter, *Documents of Jewish Sectaries*, Cambridge, 1910.

[4] Cf. Ezek. 4:5. The age of wrath began with the conquests of Nebuchadrezzar. The return from exile in 538 was never considered to be
the proper fulfilment of the great exilic and pre-exilic prophecies of
a restoration. Even Jeremiah's prophecy of a seventy-year exile is
elaborated in Dan. 9:2, 24 as a period of 490 years. The same period is
involved here in CD, since 100 years must be added (20 years of groping,
40 years for the generation of the Teacher of Righteousness, 40 years
between his death and the destruction of the enemies of the saints:
20:14f.). This gives a date of about 200 B.C. for the beginning of the
period of the Community's gestation and of about 180 for its birth when
the Teacher of Righteousness took the leadership. The gestation period
would correspond with that of the increasing hellenization in Jerusalem.
There was habitual inaccuracy at this time, however, in calculating time
intervals between the Persian and the Greek periods and the above figures
can serve only as a rough guide.

[5] The land was for the faithful. Unrighteousness and uncleanness would
lead inevitably to exile. Lev. 18:28, 26:43, Deut. 30:20.

been led astray by the Scoffer who had baptized them with
lies and obscured the ancient landmarks (i.e. moral and religious standards), thus bringing Israel into conflict with God
himself (1:13-18). The oppression and injustice practised
by the Scoffer's party aroused the anger of God so that he
treated them as unclean (1:18-21).

Those who are entering into the covenant are then addressed
and instructed concerning the ways of the wicked.[1] God acts
towards them according to wisdom, which he loves. Though
he forgives those who repent,[2] he displays great flaming
wrath by the hands of the angels of destruction towards those
who reject his commandments, whom he had not chosen from
eternity. From the beginning God knew their ways and how
long they would flourish in Israel. He has hidden his face
from the land until the end of this period, but meanwhile he
has provided for a faithful remnant which is ultimately to
fill the whole world, to whom he made known the spirit of
his holiness through his anointed prophets (2:1-13).

There follows an invitation to the faithful to be enlight-
ened so as to understand the works of God and choose what
he desires, thus resisting the guilty inclination (יצר) and
lust. They are to take warning from the punishments endured
in the past by those who followed their own will and guilty
inclination: the heavenly watchers, their children the giants,
the sons of Noah, the sons of Jacob, the Israelites at Kadesh
and those who were "the first to enter the Covenant."[3] Abra-
ham, Isaac and Jacob did not walk in the evil inclination

---

[1] Cf. the situation envisaged in 1QS 1-4.

[2] כפר construed with בעד governing the penitent, a usage characteristic
of this document, which occurs in the O.T. only at II Chron. 30:18, where
the construction reflects the priestly awareness of the gross irregularity
of the condition of the worshippers.

[3] Dupont-Sommer's rendering (*The Essene Writings*, p. 126). They are
probably the Israelite nation itself up to the time of Nebuchadrezzar
(Dupont-Sommer's first suggestion, *ibid.*, n. 1). Cf. Exod 32:27, Isa.
1:19f. for the punishment received by this group (CD 3:10f.): being
"delivered up to the sword."

and their own will, but followed God's commandments and were
counted as his friends and granted an everlasting covenant
(2:14-3:12). After those who first entered the covenant had
been delivered up to the sword, "from amongst those who clung
to the commandments of God, who survived, from amongst these
God established his covenant for Israel for ever,"[1] by revealing to them the mysteries of his will (3:12-16). Although
these covenanters defiled themselves by taking a possessive
attitude towards this revelation instead of ascribing all the
glory to God, God forgave them in his mysterious goodness[2]
and built for them a sure house[3] in Israel. Those who hold
fast to this house are destined to live for ever and all the
glory of Adam shall be theirs (3:16-20). This fulfils Ezekiel's prophecy that the priests, the Levites and the sons of
Zadok would approach God to make offerings.[4] There follows
a midrash on these terms, applying them to various elements
in the Community.[5] A list of the names and deeds of the members of the Community from its founding is then promised, but

---

[1] God's covenant with Israel does not have to be established with the
empirical Israel at any given time. If the empirical Israel is revolting
against God, he establishes Israel's covenant with the remnant of Israel.

Dupont-Sommer translates: "because of those who clung to the commandments . . .", which suggests a saving work for the remnant. The remnant
is seen, however, as a gift of God's favour (1:4) rather than as the cause
of this favour. It is by virtue of the covenant with the fathers that
God gives Israel a remnant.

[2] כפר בעד עונם וישא לפשעם (3:18). For בעד governing the sin to be forgiven *vid. supra*, p. 78. It suggests a major catastrophe. Even the remnant was ready to be lost. God's motives in forgiving them are shrouded
in mystery, since man had forfeited all claim upon him.

[3] Cf. I Sam. 2:25, where the house of Zadok is also referred to by the
same phrase.

[4] Ezek. 44:15. The "glory of Adam" was to live for ever and to approach
God. Ezekiel was constantly addressed as "son of Adam" emphasizing both
his humble position before God and his dignity before man as God's messenger (Ezek. 1:28-2:6). Cf. also I Enoch 85-90, where the white bull represents Adam and then the Messiah. Eventually all the sheep (Israel)
become white bulls.

[5] This midrash does not alter the distinction made within the Community
between priests and laity (cf. 10:4-6,13:2f.), it merely emphasizes the
priestly character of the Community as a whole.

does not appear in our texts (3:20-4:6). "These are the
first men of holiness whom God forgave, (ובכפר בעד) who justi-
fied the righteous and condemned the wicked, "and all who
come after them must act according to the interpretation of
the Law which was accepted by the original members until the
time of the final settlement, and God will pardon them too
(4:6-10).[1] When the years due for Israel's punishment have
been paid off,[2] there shall be no more being poured out[3] for
the house of Judah.[4] Instead, each man will stand on his own

---

[1]   This pardon is connected with the covenant which God made with the
first Members (4:9, cf. ברית ראשנים Lev. 26:45, *supra*, p. 88 n. 2). For
pardon in connection with the New Covenant, see Jer. 31:34 and cf. CD
8:14-18. For a discussion of the prepositions used with כפר here, see
p. 99 *infra*.

[2] והשלים הקץ ובשלים הקץ למספר השנים האלה for ובהשלים according to Rabin and
Lohse.

Habermann's reading ובשלום requires less emendation. Even if ובהשלים
is read, the thought of paying off what is due remains, since the basic
idea of שלם is the bringing about of a state of affairs in which there is
no outstanding claim on either side. This is the indispensable basis for
a proper relationship between two parties (Von Rad, *op. cit.*, I, p. 130).

[3] להשתפח. This would be the hithpa'el of שפח. The only O.T. occurrence
of this word is Isa. 3:17 where it means "smite with the scab". Rabin
thinks that there is a pun on this word here, but that the writer primarily
intended להסתפח, "to join oneself to" (so too Habermann, Vermes, Dupont-
Sommer). In the only instance of this in the O.T., however, the meaning
is not "to join", but "to continue to belong" (I Sam. 26:19).

The rendering given above is based on a reading להשתפך. The hithpa'el
of שפך occurs in Job 30:16, Lam. 2:12, 4:1. The last of these probably
forms the background here, for there we have the stones of the sanctuary
being poured out into the streets of Jerusalem. If this is the allusion,
then the following quotation from Micah is particularly apposite.

We know that ספח could be confused with שפך since LXX obviously read
משפך in Hab. 2:15 for M.T. and 1QpHab. מספח.

[4] I.e. the Jewish nation in Judaea. If the verb "joining oneself to" is
read (see previous note), the house of Judah would perhaps be some com-
promising group who were nevertheless closer to the Qumran covenanters
than the rest of the Jews (Rabin, *op. cit.*, p. 15, *ad* 4:11, n. 2). The
phrase itself, "house of Judah" also occurs in 1QpHab. 8:1, where it seems
to mean simply the Jewish nation in Judaea, and certainly cannot refer
to a group within Judaism apart from Qumran. D. Flusser has argued,
however, that the phrase is one of the Community's typological self-
designations ("Pharisees, Sadducees and Essenes in Pesher Nahum", English
summary in *Immanuel* 1 (1972), p. 39.

The usual translation could mean one of the following.

(a) At the end of the fixed period there will be no more opportunity to
join the faithful remnant. Every man must stand on his own responsibility
(watchtower).

bulwark (מצודו).[1] The wall is built, the frontier extended"
(Mic. 7:11). Until then, Belial will be let loose upon
Israel and will catch them in his three nets (מצודות): whore-
dom, wealth and defiling the sanctuary (4:10-19).

The enemies of the Community are condemned for their superficiality and immorality (4:19-21). David had an excuse for
practising polygamy, because the book of the Law was not
opened until the end of his reign. "The deeds of David rose
up (ויעלו), except for the blood of Uriah, and God left them
to him." (5:1-6)[2] The Community's enemies defile the Sanctuary
by their illicit sexual relations.[3] They defile the spirit

Besides using the verb הסתפח in a sense rather different from its only
occurrence in the O.T., this interpretation relies on the joining of two
prophetic watchman figures: Ezekiel (Ezek. 3:17) and Habakkuk (Hab. 2:1).
Only the latter is related in Hebrew to the word for a watchtower here,
and even that is doubtful (see following note).

(b) At the end of the fixed period, no one will be able to retain membership of the apostate group called "the house of Judah".

This interpretation runs counter to the use of the phrase "house of
Judah" elsewhere in the Scrolls, as we have seen.

(c) The house of Judah "has fallen and been replaced by the Community
of the Covenant, henceforth the only 'sure House in Israel'." (Dupont-
Sommer, *The Essene Writings*, p. 128, n. 2).

This interpretation involves the supposition that the end has arrived
already.

The present writer offers his own emendation with the suggestion that
it involves the fewest difficulties.

[1] The rendering "watchtower" (Lohse, Rabin, Vermes) seems to be based on
the reading מצור but מצוד was probably the original, since there is a pun
on this word in line 15, "the three nets of Belial". For the idea that
each individual will have his own source of security in the eschaton cf.
Isa. 4:5 (NEB), Mic. 4:4. In what appears to be another instance of this
phrase in 4Q 177 f 10/11:6 Allegro reads מצור (*Discoveries*, V, p. 71).
Though Lohse's rendering here is "watchtower" (*Warte*) and he sees an allusion to Hab. 2:1 (מצור), he reads מצוד in the text.

[2] Dupont-Sommer suggests that this means that the good deeds of David
rose up as an acceptable offering to God (*The Essene Writings*, p. 129
n. 6). Alternatively it may mean that David's sins rose up before God
and he overlooked them all except the matter of Uriah. This interpretation fits the context better. עלה can refer to the sin of man coming up
before God for judgement (Jon. 1:2) as well as to an offering coming up
before him. With this second interpretation there is no question of man's
acquiring merit by good deeds.

[3] Probably many of the Community's enemies were priests, but it must be
remembered that every Israelite was a part of the worshipping congregation
and responsible to maintain temple purity (Num. 19:20).

of their holiness and blaspheme against the laws of the covenant, saying that they are not valid. Whoever approaches
them will not go unpunished, unless he was forced (5:11-15).
God has already shown his wrath against these actions from
the days of Moses. Since that time the removers of bounds
led Israel astray and the land was ravaged. They preached
rebellion against the commandments given to Moses and to
God's anointed prophets (5:15-6:2). God remembered the covenant with the patriarchs and raised up wise men from Aaron
and from Israel, to whom he addressed his word: the interpretation of the Law. No revelation can be found apart from
this "until one comes who shall teach righteousness"[1] at the
end of days (6:2-11). Those who have entered the covenant
are to withdraw from the futile temple services and from all
moral and ritual evil (6:11-20). They are to care for the
members of the Community, reproving one another in love. No
one is to defile his spirit of holiness, for God has set them
apart. Everyone who lives thus in holiness shall live for
thousands of generations (6:20-7:6).[2] Those members who live
a family life in camps are still to obey the law, but those
who despise the commandments will be punished, along with
the wicked when God visits the land (7:6-10). There follows

---

[1] יורה הצדק not מורה צדק (cf. 1:11). It is not necessarily the Teacher
of Righteousness *redivivus*. Indeed, one can argue that it cannot be.
The Community is to keep to their original interpretations until the יורה
comes. These interpretations are already those of the Teacher of Righteousness and his followers. The coming of the יורה implies something
qualitatively different. The verb used, עמד, is not one of returning
(e.g. שוב). Probably both 1:11 and 6:11 allude to Hos. 10:12. In the
handwriting of the Community's scribes ויורה could easily become מורה
(cf. M.T. and LXX of Hos. 10:12). The fact that both the past event
(1:11) and the future expectation (6:11) are referred to in terms of Hos.
10:12 should warn us against thinking of the Teacher of Righteousness
exclusively in terms of one historical figure. His successors may have
been referred to by the same term under the influences of the same scrip-
ture. If this was the case, the Community would not need the concept of
a Teacher of Righteousness *redivivus*. See Black, *The Dead Sea Scrolls
and Christian Doctrine*, pp. 9-11.

[2] Ms. B, 19:2, has a reference to Deut. 7:9. God's promises of earthly
blessings are extended towards an eternal future in the inter-testamental
literature. In this document one can see the development in process (cf.
3:20).

a midrash upon Isa. 7:17 and Amos 5:26f., which are interpreted in connection with the history of the Community, There
seems to be a distinction between the interpreter of the Law,
presumably the Teacher of Righteousness "who came" (or, "who
would come") "to Damascus" and the prince of the whole congregation "who shall smite the children of Seth" (presumably
the Messiah of Israel, 7:10-21). As it was during the former
visitation, so shall it be at the next: the faithful will be
saved but the apostates given up to the sword of Belial (7:21-
8:2).[1] The rulers of Israel had sinned in their greed for
wealth, injustice, perverseness and failure to keep themselves separate from the ungodly masses and their ways (8:4-
10). The kings of the nations and the chief of the kings
of Greece were to take vengeance on them, but those who plas-
tered the wall[2] did not perceive this, because a deceiving
preacher had persuaded them otherwise (8:10-13). Just as
God loved Israel, not because of her righteousness, but because of his oath to the fathers (Deut. 7:8, 9:5), so he will
love those who follow after the first generation of covenanters, who testified against their unrighteous contemporaries
(8:14-18). "None of the men who enter the New Covenant in the
land of Damascus, and who again betray it and depart from the
fountain of living waters, shall be reckoned with the Council
of the people or inscribed in its Book from the day of the
gathering in of the Teacher of the Community until the coming
of the Messiah out of Aaron and Israel" (19:32-20:1).[3] The
Member who fails to perform his duty though lack of courage
shall be expelled temporarily, until he returns to a state of
perfect holiness. Meanwhile, let no one consort with him, for
all the angels have cursed him (20:2-8). There is no place

---

[1]   Ms. B (19:11-13) quotes Ezek. 9:4 here. The "former visitation" would
then be whatever visitation the author thought Ezekiel was prophesying
about. This could be either the destruction of Jerusalem by Nebuchadrezzar
(cf. 1:5f.), or some event in more recent history. According to Dupont-
Sommer this was the capture of Jerusalem by Pompey in 63 B.C. (*The Essene
Writings*, p. 135 n. 1).

[2]   The allusion is to Ezek. 13:10 as also in 4:19. The reference is to
the superficiality of the Community's enemies. They did not perceive
Israel's real problems, but were content to "paper over the cracks".

[3]   Vermes's rendering, *op. cit.*, p. 106.

in the house of the Law for those who have rejected the pre-
cepts, set idols upon their heart and despised the new covenant[1] made in the land of Damascus; nor is there any place
for their families (20:8-13).

"From the day of the gathering in of the Teacher of the
Community until the end of all the men of war who deserted
to the Liar there shall pass about forty years . . . But
those who turn from the sin of Jacob, who keep the Covenant
of God, shall then speak each man to his fellow, to justify
each man his brother,[2] that their step may take the way of
God.[3] And God will heed their words and will hear, and a book
of reminder shall be written before Him of them that fear
God and worship His name, against the time when salvation and
righteousness shall be revealed to them that fear God."[4] Then
one will be able to discern between the just and the unjust
and to a thousand generations God will show mercy to those

---

[1] The text emphatically states that the covenant made in the land of
Damascus is the new covenant. The new covenant promised in Jer. 31:31ff.
is clearly meant, but there is no quotation of the Jeremiah passage. It
influenced the writer's thinking on the following points.

(a) Israel had broken the covenant made at the Exodus (vs. 32).
(b) Knowledge of the Law is important (vs. 33).
(c) God will forgive the members of the new covenant (vs. 34).

The radical implication that the heart of man and the Law of God are no
longer to be separate entities, thus doing away with the very idea of
obedience to an external norm (heteronomy) was completely missed by Qumran (see Von Rad, *op. cit.*, II, pp. 213ff.).

[2] I.e. to declare him just. There is no clear case in the O.T. where
the hiph'il of צדק means simply "to make someone righteous" or "to turn
someone to righteousness". The reference most likely to bear the latter
sense, Dan. 12:3, is capable of being translated "those who justify many",
as an allusion to Isa. 53:11, where the meaning is that the Servant will
gain for the "many" a verdict of "not guilty" in the great law process
which God has with his people. Ecclus. 42:2, the other instance adduced
by Rabin in favour of his translation "to make righteous" (*The Zadokite
Documents*, p. 41, *ad* 20:18, n. 2), is translated "acquit" in the NEB.
In the present context, however, and in the context of the Qumran theology, it is very probable that this justification is to be achieved by
making the members practically just through reproof and the discipline
of the Community. "Turn them to justice", therefore, describes what
happens, but the purpose of this action is to make them just before God.

[3] Literally "in order to support their steps in the way of God". The
acquittal before God's tribunal was to be a support for a subsequent life
of holiness. Cf. 1QS 11:13-15 for a similar situation (*vid. supra*, p. 79).

[4] Vermes's translation (*op. cit.*, p. 107).

who love him (20:13-22). There follows an obscure passage
which Habermann does not venture to point, but which seems to
affirm that some who were faithful to God left the holy city
at the time when Israel sinned and defiled the Temple (20:22-
24). The members of the covenant who transgressed the Law
will be cut off from the camp when God's glory appears to
Israel, as well as all those who do evil in Judah (or "to
Judah", 20:24-27). As for those who heed the Law and the
Community's regulations, confess their own and their fathers'
sins and the justice of God's punishment of them, and are cor-
rected by the former judgements which the members of the Community have undergone, they will rejoice and overcome all men,
God will forgive (כפר בעד) them and they will see his salvation
(20:27-34).

The laws of the Community follow. The following points are
relevant for its soteriology.

"No man over the age of sixty shall hold office as a Judge
of the Congregation, for 'because man sinned his days have been
shortened and in the heat of His anger against the in-
habitants of the earth God ordained that their understanding
should depart even before their days are completed' (Jubilees
xxiii, 11)."[1]

The duties of the *Mebaqqer* (camp overseer) are clearly
pastoral. He is to instruct the congregation in the works
of God, love them as a father or a shepherd and loosen all
the fetters which bind them. He alone is to admit postulants,
examining each man according to his spiritual and material
capacity and assigning him a position in the Community accordingly (13:7-13).

"And this is the exact statement of the rulings in which
[they shall walk during the epoch of wickedness, until there
shall arise the Messiah of Aaron and Israel, and he will
make conciliation for their trespass . . . ." (14:18f).[2]

---

[1]   10:7-10. Vermes's translation (*op. cit.*, p. 111).

[2]   Rabin's translation (*The Zadokite Documents*, p. 70).

The lacuna has been filled with the usual phrases occurring
in CD in this kind of context. Ginzberg restores, "until God
sends the Messiah"[1] thus avoiding any atoning work for the
Messiah, but the phrase "until the coming of the Messiah of
Aaron and Israel" (with slight variations) occurs in 19:10f.,
20:1 and 12:23f. and is, therefore, the most likely conject-
ure.

The Old Testament background is clearly Dan. 9:24, where
there is a combination of the rare construction of כפר without a following preposition[2] and the concept of anointing.
Qumran probably understood this passage to mean that after a
period of 490 years Israel's iniquity would be forgiven and
she would be delivered from her oppressors with the coming
of the Messiah. In the present passage the coming of the Messiah and the eschatological forgiveness are so closely linked
that the latter can be spoken of as the purpose of the former.[3]
This passage does not imply that the Messiah will make atonement, but only that his coming is God's final act in forgiving
Israel.[4]

F. SUMMARY OF QUMRAN ATONEMENT IN THE HASMONÆAN PERIOD

In 1QS 9:3-6 the Community atones for sin by the spirit of
holiness fostered in its midst through its discipline which
forms a foundation upon which other penitents may be built
like the stones of the Temple. The atonement is for the bene-

---

[1] Rabin, *The Zadokite Documents*, p. 71, *ad* 14:19, n. 1.

[2] Although in the O.T. as a whole כפר is rarely followed by no preposition
to designate the sins atoned for, in the prophecy of Isaiah this is the
only usage (Isa. 47:11, and with the corresponding passive construction:
6:7, 22:14, 27:9). This fact may have determined its use in Dan. 9.24.
We know that the author of Daniel studied the earlier prophets (Dan. 9:2).

[3] ויכפר. Simple *waw* with the imperfective usually expresses purpose.

[4] The Messiah forgives Israel in that he effectively assures her of God's
pardon by delivering her from gentile oppression and pollution. Cf. the
usage in 4Q Nab., *supra*, p. 12.

Black's suggestion (*The Dead Sea Scrolls and Christian Doctrine*, p. 14),
that it refers to cultic atonement, is rendered rather improbable by the
lack of either of the usual cultic prepositions: על, בעד. Cf. 1QM 2:5.

fit of the Holy Land. This is not connected with the punishment of the wicked as it was in 1QS 8:6f., 10, but rather with
the discipline of the Members. The temple imagery is somewhat
more pronounced than in 1QS 8:1-11 and extends even to the
preposition used with the verb "atone".[1] The reality which is
described under this metaphor of an expiatory oblation, however, is the provision of an opportunity for repentance by
the existence of a faithful remnant.

1QSa 1:3 makes it clear when this repentance was expected to
take place on a scale large enough to bring Israel a definitive
salvation. This was to be in the last days when the Messiahs
of Aaron and Israel would lead the repentant nation to victory.
Then the atonement which was the purpose of the Community's
existence would issue in deliverance for Israel.

1QSb and 4Q Test. show that the idea of the efficacy of
cultic atonement and the stress on the punishment of the wicked
as a means of salvation are still important elements in the
Community's thinking.

G. SUMMARY OF ATONEMENT IN CD

Except for 14:19, CD always has God as the subject of the
atoning action. The verb is usually followed by בעד with the
person to be forgiven.[2] This usage is probably modelled on
II Chron. 30:18, the only instance in the Old Testament where,
with God as the subject and man the beneficiary of the atoning
action, the verb is used with the preposition בעד. This is
even more clear than the case of 1QS 11:14.[3] Adoption of this
usage indicates the Community's awareness that Israel's standing before God was highly irregular and any forgiveness she obtained would be entirely by God's mysterious grace, since there
was no more provision for atonement, whether in cult or covenant. In 3:18 this usage is extended by the use of this preposition with the sins to be forgiven.[4]

---

[1] *Supra*, p. 84 n. 2.

[2] CD 2:5, 4:6f., 10, 20:34.

[3] *Vid. supra*, pp. 78f.

[4] *Vid. supra*, p. 90 n. 2.

In 4:9 we have כפר על with the sins to be forgiven. This
construction occurs alongside of בעד with the persons forgiven.
The writer is clearly not using these terms carelessly. כפר
על is found with God as the subject in Jer. 18:23 and Ps. 79:9.
The latter probably forms the background here, since Ps. 79 is
concerned with the defilement of the temple and the desolation
of Jerusalem, a passage linked in the writer's mind probably
with Lam. 4, which we have argued is also part of the background of this passage.[1] The same construction is taken up
again in 1QS 9:4, where, however, God is not the subject of
the atoning action.[2]

In the only other occurrence of כפר in CD (14:19) no preposition follows. The usage here is probably influenced by
Dan. 9:24. The 1QS examples of this construction (2:8 and
3:8) seem not to be imitations of CD, but rather to reflect
Isa. 22:14 and Prov. 16:6 respectively.

In CD there is no stress on the spirit as a means of salvation. If there is any objective basis for forgiveness, it is
the covenant (4:9f.), but this is constantly being broken and
the only real basis is God's own forgiving nature (2:5) and his
free grace which is reflected in the construction most used
with the verb "atone". The idea of the Community's existence
constituting a saving foundation for the rest of Israel is
also absent from CD. Indeed, the idea of a future mass conversion of Israel is no longer emphasised but rather that some
members of the Community may be lost in the last days (20:24-
27). The work contains a typical doxology of judgement in the
style of Dan. 9 (20:27-34).

God is the subject of the atoning action throughout, except
for 14:19, where it is the Messiah. Even here, however, the
Messianic atonement seems to mean only that the coming of the
Messiah is a sign that God has forgiven Israel in accordance
with the programme outlined in Dan. 9:24.

---

[1] *Vid. supra*, p. 91 n. 3.

[2] *Vid. supra*, pp. 71f.

CHAPTER V: ATONEMENT IN THE REMAINING SCROLLS

A. ATONEMENT IN 1QM

The first part of this chapter will be devoted to those
Scrolls which Starcky[1] has dated in the "Herodian" period:
1QM, 1QpHab., 4Q Flor., 4QpPs. 37, 4QpIsa., 4Q Patr. Bl.
The second part will treat the Scrolls not dated by Starcky.

The present text of the War Scroll (1QM) has probably developed from a tradition originating at the time of the
Maccabaean Revolt.[2] This theory would allow for the modern-
ization of military terms to correspond with the Roman situation.[3]

The main point of the book is salvation in the original
sense of the word: deliverance from enemies. The foes here
are sinners led on by Belial. The final victory over them
is to come after a protracted eschatological war which is to
be a holy war under the direction of the priests. It is to be
a real conflict, for some of the righteous will be killed in
battle (16:9ff.).[4] Yet the main interest of the document is
not in strategy and tactics, but in the holy-war character of
the conflict by virtue of which victory is assured for the
Sons of Light. The fighters confess that they are unworthy
of this because of their sins (11:4) and that God has given
them the victory for the sake of his covenant with his people
and for his own name's sake (18:7f.).[5] Priestly activity is
very prominent throughout the campaigns. It is the priests
who are to direct the movements of the troops by making dif-

---

[1] *Op. cit.*, pp. 500f.

[2] J. Van Der Ploeg, *Le rouleau de la guerre*, Leiden, 1959, pp. 22-25.

[3] According to the thesis sustained by Y. Yadin, *The Scroll of the War
of the Sons of Light against the Sons of Darkness*, London, 1962.

[4] Cf. Num. 31:49 in the sequel to the Phinehas story.

[5] In this connection God is called the "God of justice (צדק)", another
instance of God's saving justice being referred to by this term.

ferent sounds on the trumpets (7:8-9:9)[1] and all the time
regular Temple sacrifices are to be kept up as the priests
"stand by at the burnt-offerings and the sacrifices, to set
out the incense offering of sweet savour for the pleasure of
God, to atone for all His congregation" (2:5).[2] The priests
are also to be fed continually before him at the table of
glory.[3] This mention of feeding in close connection with
atonement is perhaps a reference to the eating of the sin
offering. It is clear that cultic atonement had not been
abandoned by Qumran, but merely postponed until the last day.
There is no theory of the *modus operandi* of this kind of atonement. The construction used with כפר here, בעד governing the
people atoned for, is the usual expression in connection with
solemn national atonement rituals (Lev. 9:7, ch. 16 *passim*,
Ezek. 45:17).

This final war is to be unleashed "when the exiles of the
Sons of Light return from the Wilderness of the Nations to
encamp in the Wilderness of Jerusalem."[4] "The wilderness of
the nations" is a phrase borrowed from Ezek. 20:35, as Yadin
has noted. The way the phrase is used in 1QM shows that the
whole context of Ezek. 20 was in the mind of the author, for
he speaks of returning from this wilderness, whereas Ezek. 20:
35 says that God will bring Israel into it. It is not until
later (verse 42) that a return from the wilderness into the
Promised Land is mentioned. The prophet seems to be saying
that Israel will not be allowed simply to settle down in ex-

---

[1] Cf. Num. 31:6.

[2] Yadin's translation.

[3] Yadin translates: "and bring fat sacrifices before him", but in 1QS
10:15 and 1QH 10:26 להדשן means "enjoy food" not "give food" and this
furnishes the best clue to the meaning here, since it is exactly the same
phrase and the phrase is rare.

[4] 1:3, Yadin's translation. For a fragment of a similar phrase see
4QpIsa.[a] f 5/6:2, *Discoveries*, V, pp. 12f.

Whether or not, as W.D. Davies has suggested (*The Gospel and the Land*,
Berkeley, c. 1974, p. 103), the Qumran "exiles" were linked somehow with
Babylonian Jewry, there remains an important theological sense in which
they regarded themselves as exiles (*vid. supra*, p. 10). See also Jaubert's
explanation in terms of a faithful remnant: "Le pays de Damas," *Rev. Bib.*,
65 (1958), pp. 214-248.

ilic conditions, adapting to the gentile way of life (vs. 32),
but that God will bring her back to the Promised Land through
the wilderness, like a second exodus. This second wilderness
experience is called "the wilderness of the peoples" in parallel with the "wilderness of the land of Egypt" (vs. 36) which
means only "the wilderness through which Israel passed when
they left the land of Egypt" (cf. vs. 10). Consequently "the
wilderness of the nations" means "the wilderness through which
God will bring Israel when he brings her out of her exile
amongst the nations." During the second wilderness experience
God promises, "I will cause you to pass under the rod, and I
will bring you into the bond of the covenant; and I will purge
out from among you the rebels, and them that transgress
against me" (vss. 37f.). This is clearly a blue-print for
Qumran.

According to Yadin the phrase "the wilderness of Jerusalem"
does not occur in the Old Testament. He suggests Isa. 52:9
and 64:10 (64:9 Heb.). The latter is particularly striking.
It serves to illustrate the link in thought between the noun
מדבר (wilderness) and the root שמם (makc desolate) and points
to the importance in the Community's thinking of the whole
theme of the Exile and of the desolation of the Holy Land as
it was classically enunciated in Lev. 26:31ff. and re-interpreted in terms of gentile pollution in Dan. 8:13, 9:27, 11:31
and 12:11. The term "wilderness of Jerusalem" means simply
the polluted city which is to be cleansed by force of arms
from contamination by gentiles and their allies within Israel.[1]

B. 1QpHAB.

The Scroll mainly concerns the enemies of the Community
and of Israel. It envisages punishment for the wicked in
this life as well as an eschatological judgement of fire (e.g.
10:5). Escape from this is by obeying the Law and believing
in the Teacher of Righteousness (8:1-3), waiting patiently
for the appointed time of deliverance (7:9-14). Their patience

---

[1] So B. Jongeling, *Le rouleau de la guerre*, Assen, 1962, p. 55.

will be rewarded when God takes pity on them and commits to
them the task of executing judgement upon the wicked who have
distressed them (5:3-6).[1] The motive for God's kindness to
the righteous is probably his habitual sympathy for the oppressed and championship of their cause.[2]

C. SMALLER SCROLLS OF THE HERODIAN PERIOD

  4Q Florilegium[3] consists of a collection of texts concerning
the Community and the Messiah of David. The two are very
closely linked and Ps. 2:1 is interpreted as referring to the
opposition to the "elect ones of Israel" in the last days,
that is to the Community (1:19). The Community is presented
as a sanctuary of men which is to last for ever "that there
they may send up, like the smoke of incense, the works of the
Law."[4] Nothing is stated, however, about whether these works
would atone for others, like the incense offered by Aaron to
stay the plague in Num. 16:46f. The accent is not on atoning
for sin in this passage, but on the exclusion of sinners from
the sanctuary, thus bringing to an end the "desolation" of the
exilic time of judgement.[5]

  4QpPs. 37[6] takes the sayings of Ps. 37 about the righteous
and the wicked and applies them to the Teacher of Righteousness
and his enemies respectively. The material blessings promised
for the righteous are readily appropriated by the Community
for its members. There is no attempt to spiritualize them.
The wicked are to be utterly exterminated and the righteous
will grow fat on all the luxuries of the flesh.[7] They will

---

[1] I translate 5:4-6 "and by their chastisement (i.e. that meted out by
the elect) shall all the wicked ones of his people receive the punishment
due for their guilt on whose account they (i.e. the elect) suffered distress in keeping his commandments." אשם sometimes means "suffer punishment"
(G. Lisowsky, Konkordanz zum hebräischen alten Testament, Stuttgart, 1964,
pp. 170f.). אשר . . . למו surely means pro quibus.

[2] Cf. 12:2-10.

[3] Discoveries, V, pp. 53ff.

[4] 1:5-7, Vermes's translation.

[5] 1:5. Vid. supra, p. 80 n. 1, p. 102.

[6] Discoveries, V, pp. 42ff.

[7] 2:10. Dupont-Sommer 1:10.

live a thousand generations and all the inheritance of Adam
will be theirs and their descendants'.[1] These are the meek
who will possess the land because they accept the time of
affliction.[2]

The commentary on Isaiah (4QpIsa.)[3] is very fragmentary and
the comments seem to have been short and mainly concerned
with identifying figures in the text with the Community or
its enemies. There is very little of soteriological significance and passages of Isaiah which are rich in this respect
are not elaborated for their salvation doctrine.[4] It is
tempting to speculate that a Qumran commentary on Isaiah 53
would turn out to be equally arid. The word כפרם occurs in
the fragment 4QpIsa[c] f 14:5 which is probably a comment on
Isa. 29:14, but the passage is far too fragmentary to draw
any soteriological conclusions from it.

4Q Patriarchal Blessings is a small fragment containing
a commentary on Gen. 49:10. The enigmatic "Shiloh" in that
verse is interpreted as the "Messiah of Righteousness, the
Branch of David; for to him and to his seed has been given the
Covenant of the kingship of his people for everlasting generations, because he kept [. . .] the Law with the members of
the Community."[5] This seems to mean that the Messiah of David
is to emerge from the Community itself. He does not appear
to be a supernatural figure, for he has descendants like any
other man. It is clear that the coming of the Messiah does
not herald the end of the world.[6] The same perseverance in

---

[1]   3:1f., Dupont-Sommer 2:1f.

[2]   The manuscript is difficult to read at this point. Allegro reads התעות
and translates "error", Lohse has התענית which he renders "Qual". The
latter occurs in Ezra 9:5 in connection with Ezra's doxology of judgement.
The word for "accept" is קבל as in Job 2:10, not רצה as in Lev. 26. See
the discussion by Robert B. Coote, "'MW‹D HT‹NYT' in 4Q 171 (pesher Psalm
37), fragments 1-2, col II, line 9," *Rev. Qum.*, 8 (1972), pp. 81-85.

[3]   *Discoveries*, V, pp. 11ff.

[4]   E.g. 4QpIsa[a] f 8/10:11-24 *ad* Isa. 9:1-3; 4QpIsa[c] 2:3ff. *ad* Isa. 30:15ff.

[5]   Dupont-Sommer's translation, *The Essene Writings*, p. 315.

[6]   See Carmignac, "La notion d'eschatologie dans la Bible et à Qumrân,"
Rev. Qum. 7 (Dec. 1969), pp. 17-31.

righteousness which wins for the Members the right to execute
God's judgement upon the sinners, their enemies, is to win
this same right for the Messiah who will emerge as their
leader.[1]

D. SUMMARY OF QUMRAN SALVATION IDEAS IN THE HERODIAN PERIOD

   There is considerable concern about salvation from gentile
oppression and pollution. The exilic motif of the desolation
of the land continues. Material blessings figure as important
elements amongst the benefits of salvation. A sense of sin
is evinced in the battle confessions of 1QM. God's forgiveness seems to be motivated by his pity of the Covenanters
suffering in exile. Their patience in obeying the Law in the
face of difficulties will be rewarded when they are called
upon to execute God's vengeance upon the sinners who had formerly distressed them in their life of obedience. This faithfulness to the Law is spoken of as a sacrifice well pleasing
to God. The Messiah himself is to emerge from the midst of
this suffering and submissive community and be rewarded by
the leadership in the final war to exterminate evil. In the
last days atonement rites are to be resumed in the Temple by
the rightful priests. They will be efficacious.[2]

   Some of these ideas could have provided a fertile soil for
legalism: patience being rewarded by an avenging role, the
works of the Law as sacrifices, material blessings as salvation. If the idea of merit could have entered the Community's
thinking through these doors, it is even more certain that the
idea of a pool of merits for the benefit of their erring
fellow Israelites would be excluded. In this period there
seems to be even less concern for outsiders than before.

   Since the Messiah is so closely linked with the Community he
could even have been a suffering Messiah, but his sufferings
would not have been atoning. They would simply qualify him

---

[1]   Cf. 1QpHab. 5:3-6. *Vid. supra*, pp. 102f.

[2]   Presumably they are to be continued to an indefinite future, but their
purpose would not be to expiate thorough-going wickedness, since this will
have ceased to exist through the destruction of the wicked.

to take vengeance on his enemies.

It could be argued that this rather harsh picture of Qumran religion in this period results from the genres of the material studied: directions for a holy war and pesharim. Surely the hymns of 1QH were still being sung as well as the biblical Psalms! Surely the solemn words of the covenant blessings and curses were still being spoken to shake the Members out of any complacency they may have developed! One must answer that the material studied here has been dated from this period with reasonable certainty and 1QH, 1QS and CD from an earlier period with the same degree of certainty, if not greater. Judgements can be formed only upon the material available and the writer feels he must accept this until more scrolls are discovered and published. If the genres concerned are so unsuitable for soteriological content, it still remains a fact that this period found these genres congenial. Since this period begins roughly about the same time as the birth of Christ, this material forms part of the background to the ministry of Jesus![1]

E. MISCELLANEOUS SCROLLS

The Angelic Liturgy (4Q Sl. 39)[2] is a series of beatitudes spoken on the faithful by angelic princes. The upright, the pure, the wise and the perfect are to be blessed with spiritual blessings: everlasting peace and the favour of God. The material has affinities with some of the hymns and with the blessings of 1QS. The date of composition could well be early.

1Q 34 and 34 *bis*[3] contains a collection of liturgical prayers, but it is rather fragmentary. The "faithful shepherd" in 2:8 may be a reference to the founder of the Community. There is a fragment of the beginning of a prayer for the Day of Atonement, but it is difficult to see whether any of the other fragments contains a continuation of this prayer. The

---

[1] See Starcky, *op. cit.*, p. 499.

[2] Vermes, *op. cit.*, pp. 210ff. Dupont-Sommer, *The Essene Writings*, pp. 330ff.

[3] *Discoveries*, I, pp. 136, 152ff.

root כפר occurs in the saying in 1:5f. that God has given the
wicked as a ransom (כופר) for the elect.[1] Presumably this
includes the wicked within Israel as well as the gentiles.

1Q Myst.[2] has affinities with 1QH 11:15-22 and 1QS 4:18f.
It declares that there will be an end to wickedness as darkness is dispelled by the rising sun. The fact that evil is
practised in every nation, though all men loathe it, is evidence that it must come to an end one day. The means by which
this is to be accomplished seems to be an eternal imprisonment of those who are begotten of wickedness (1:5). This
perhaps refers to the spirits of the giants who are leading
men astray according to I Enoch 16, 19, until they are confin-
ed along with the Watchers who have begotten them (I Enoch
10-11).

11Q Melch.[3] contains commentaries on a collection of texts
centring on a messianic figure who is symbolically[4] referred
to as Melchizedek. The texts interpreted are mainly passages
from the Pentateuch about the law of jubilee, from the Psalms
about justice in trying lawsuits and from Isaiah about the
proclamation of the coming liberation. Lines 7f. are particularly interesting. Carmignac translates: "le dixième
jubilé pour faire l'expiation en ce (temps-là) sur tous
[tes (?)] fils [, su]r les homm[es de] ton parti". The tenth
jubilee is probably the end of the period of 490 years after
Nebuchadrezzar. In the light of Dan. 9:24 it is not surpris-
ing to read of atonement in this connection. Unfortunately
the lacuna leaves it uncertain whether it is Melchizedek or
simply the passage of time that is to effect the atonement.
The Hebrew reads: לכפר בו על כול בני. ⅃ is the usual pro-

---

[1] Cf. Isa. 43:3.

[2] *Discoveries*, I, pp. 102ff. 1Q Myst. f 6:2 has כפר construed with על
governing the sin and the next line has it construed with some direct object. These lines appear to be using the language of cultic atonement
(cf. Lev. 5:18, Ezek. 43:20), to express metaphorically the final conquest
of evil in the universe.

[3] See Carmignac, "Le document de Qumran sur Melkisédeq," *Rev. Qum.*, 7
(Dec., 1970), pp. 343-378.

[4] *Ibid.*, p. 369.

position employed after כפר to indicate the means of atonement.
על governing the person to be atoned for is the standard usage
in Old Testament cultic texts. In the Scrolls it only occurs
in this instance. Is Melchizedek a figure of a priestly Messiah who will make cultic atonement for the faithful remnant
in Israel, or is the language of cultic atonement being used
here metaphorically for the forgiveness which will come to the
faithful remnant when the period of trial for Israel is at an
end? Our present text is too fragmentary to yield an answer.

Starcky's article also mentions a manuscript from Cave 4
which he has provisionally coded 4QAhA, because it seems to
refer to an Aaronic figure of the future.[1] The work seems
to belong to a Testament of Jacob in which the patriarch speaks
to his son Levi of an eschatological figure who is certainly
a high priest of the messianic era. "Il fera l'expiation
(ykpr) pour tous les fils de sa génération et il sera envoyé
à tous les fils de son [   ]." His wisdom will be great but
he will have to suffer through the opposition of his enemies:
"Ils auront pour lui des paroles de mépris et ils le couvrir-
ont de honte; ils rendront ta face (à toi Lévi) haïssable
[   ] et il sera entouré de tromperie et de violence (wbšqr
wḥms mqmh); le peuple errera en ses jours et seront abandonnés
. . . ." Starcky is not convinced that the allusions are to the
sufferings of the founder of the Community. He thinks that
there is an identification of the Aaronic high priest with the
Servant of Yahweh, but cautions: "aucune des expressions em-
ployées en 4QAhA n'indique que les souffrances de ce messie
ont une valeur rédemptrice pour le peuple."

Since publishing this article, Abbé Starcky has written out
the text of this fragment and sent it to the writer. The document is in Aramaic and the only common vocabulary with Isa. 53
is the term חמס ("violence", cf. Isa. 53:9) and the imperfective יטעה (equivalent to the verb תעה "have gone astray" in
53:6). Now חמס is not a rare word and the context in Isa. 53
is quite unlike that in this document. Furthermore, the link
with שקר ("deceit", but not the word used in Isa. 53:9) sug-

_____
[1] *Rev. Bib.*, 70 (1963), p. 492.

gests that the background is Hab. 2:17f., where both these
words occur and which we know from 1QpHab. 12 to have been
applied by the Community to their own situation. As for חעה,
the word is not rare and other background passages are equally
or even more likely. Ezek. 44:15 is particularly noteworthy:
because the Zadokites were faithful when the rest of Israel
went astray, they will be granted the priestly functions at
the Restoration. This accords well with the theme of a high-
priestly figure which is being presented here. The preposition
used after the verb יכפר is על, as is common in Levitical usage
to denote a cultic atonement (כפר plus על governing the person
occurs about fifty times in the priestly literature of the Old
Testament).

The opposition which the Aaronic priest is to suffer is probably an expression of his solidarity with the Community and
is analogous to the solidarity of the Davidic Messiah with the
Community, which we have seen to be a feature of the Herodian
period at Qumran.[1] If this is the case, the Aaronic high priest
may have earned, by his suffering with the Community from whose
midst he was expected to emerge, the right to bring atonement,
either through the cult or by ridding the land of its oppressors.[2]

1Q DM is an apocryphal little Deuteronomy, mainly concerned
with the sabbatical year and the Day of Atonement, which may
be linked together in the Community's thinking.[3] In 3:11,
where the subject is clearly the Day of Atonement, we have כפר
in the pu'al used absolutely. The same verb also occurs in
4:3, where many lacunae make the context harder to interpret.
There is mention of something being shed on the earth, presumably bllod. The verb is again in the pu'al, but this time
construed with ל governing "them" and ב governing "it". The
usage here seems to correspond most closely to Deut. 21:8.

---

[1] *Vid. supra*, pp. 105f. Starcky places 4QAhA in the Hasmonæan era.

[2] Cf. Black's view that the Community's leaders, the "Rightful Teachers",
were in fact a succession of priestly messianic pretenders (*The Dead Sea
Scrolls and Christian Doctrine*, pp. 4-11).

[3] *Discoveries*, I, pp. 91ff.

One is tempted to interpret this as meaning, "blood guilt
will be forgiven them by this means (pouring out the blood
in the act of secular slaughter)". This would involve a
harmonizing of the teaching of Lev. 17:4 with Deut. 12:21-25,
in the light of Deut. 21:1-9. Although this fits in with the
immediately preceding context, however, it hardly accords with
the remainder of the column which concerns the Day of Atonement rites.

In the rest of the fragmentary material, published in *Discoveries in the Judaean Desert*, a dominant theme is the Exile
and Return. There are fragments of apocryphal prophecies
containing warnings of the distress which is to come upon
Israel in the exilic period as a result of her unfaithfulness.
The style recalls the curses of Deuteronomy and the threats
of Lev. 26.[1] There are also fragments of works containing
visions of the New Jerusalem in the style of Ezekiel.[2]

The theme of the Community's future function of punishing
the wicked is perhaps intimated by the mention of Phinehas in
6Q13[3] and perhaps of the execution of judgement by the Levites
and of their separation from the guilty in Israel in 4Q159 f 5.[4]

1QpMic. f 8/10:6-8[5] promises salvation in the day of judgement for those who join the Community. 4Q177 1:5[6] refers to
ten righteous men in the city, clearly alluding to Gen. 18:32.
If the Community considered itself to be fulfilling the function of the ten righteous within Israel, this must be interpreted in the light of everything else we know about its
soteriology. The salvation it would achieve on the basis of
the principle of solidarity would be of no avail for the
wicked in the land nor could it delay the fixed times of God's

---

[1] See 1Q25 (*ibid.*, pp. 100f.), 2Q23 (*ibid.*, III, pp. 82f.), 3Q5 (*ibid.*,
pp. 96f.), 5Q14 (*ibid.*, pp. 183f.), 4Q179 (*ibid.*, V, pp. 76ff.), 4Q182
2:7 (עוונם את ויוצר), *ibid.*, p. 81).

[2] E.g. 1Q32 (*ibid.*, I, pp. 134f.), 2Q24 (*ibid.*, III, pp. 85-89), 5Q15
(*ibid.*, p. 184).

[3] *Ibid.*, pp. 126f.

[4] *Ibid.*, V, pp. 8f.

[5] *Ibid.*, I, p. 78.

[6] *Ibid.*, V, pp. 71f.

visitations. Its effect would be to provide a concrete opportunity for repentance and to ensure a glorious future for
the land and for the purged remnant who would inherit it.
Gen. 18:32 could not cancel out Ezek. 14:16 in the thinking
of a group which took seriously the ideal of Exod. 32:29.

4Q159 (4Q Ord)[1] is a commentary on the laws concerning provision for the poor in connection with harvesting practices
and on the law of the half shekel. The phrase "to atone for
(ל) your sins" occurs in 2:2. The context is rather fragmentary but the atonement seems to be obtained by the kind treatment of the poor. The construction used, ל governing the sins
to be atoned for, seems to be used in this way only here.[2]
It is theoretically possible that the reference is to the
atonement money mentioned in 2:6 (the כופר). It is also probable that the Community linked the Day of Atonement, the
sabbatical year and the year of jubilee in its thinking[3] and
an explanation might be conjectured on this basis. In the
absence of a firmer text one is unfortunately reduced to
guesswork.

Eternal double predestination is taught in 4Q181 f 1[4] and
the doctrine of the two spirits is taken so far as to give
the actual mathematical proportions of the spirits of light
and of darkness in the individual whose horoscope has survived
in 4Q186.[5]

---

[1] *Ibid.*, pp. 6f.

[2] But cf. Num. 35:33 and 1QH 15:24, which are somewhat similar.

[3] Cf. 1Q DM 3:6f., *Discoveries*, I, pp. 94f.; 11Q Melch. *passim.*

[4] *Discoveries*, V. pp. 79f.

[5] *Ibid.*, pp. 88ff.

SUMMARY AND CONCLUSIONS

A. GENERAL

Since the present work has used a textual and chronological
approach to the material, the main conclusions reached as a
result of the study will now be presented thematically.
Where there is reason to suppose that Qumran thinking on a
point of soteriology underwent development, this will be
indicated. Otherwise it is to be assumed that the view in
question was held throughout the history of the Community.

For the Qumran covenanters, God has a dispute with the
whole human race in which mankind is in the wrong and God in
the right. Man's appropriate response to this situation is
to take sides with God's justice against sinful mankind including one's self, submitting to God's just punishment and
accepting with gratitude any favour God may graciously bestow.
In the early period it was emphasized that even this response
is itself a gift from God and as such pleasing to him, so that
it could be spoken of metaphorically as an atonement. The men
of Qumran aimed to display perfectly this spirit of acceptance
and in the period of their early zeal they succeeded to the
point where it is at times difficult to see whether they were
speaking of salvation or of condemnation when they mentioned
the judgement and the righteousness of God.

Apart from one of the Member hymns (21 T), the suffering of
the world around them gave no concern to these covenanters.
Indeed, they cursed rather than loved the renegade and the reprobate. Thus they sought to reflect God's attitude to the
wicked.

They believed evil would come to an end. The question of
whether this involved a denial of eternal punishment seems
not to have occurred to them. They regarded the punishment of
the wicked as an unmitigated good, since God is glorified in
it. In the early documents the Community is seen as a source

of salvation for the masses of Israel. They are to be saved
through joining it. In CD and afterwards this idea seems to
have been eclipsed.

In CD the emphasis on the Community as a foundation for
future Members is replaced by the remnant idea. Already in
1QS 9:3-6 there had been stress on the thought that the whole
life of the faithful would please God like a sacrifice of
atonement. The effect would be blessing for the land. The
idea is based on corporate thinking which had remained strong
even after Ezekiel's forcible proclamation of individual responsibility. The Essenes continued the post-exilic practice
of confessing their ancestors' sins along with their own.

B. SIN AND PUNISHMENT

As in the Old Testament God punishes through the circumstances of life: through sickness and the sword. The Founder
himself suffered disease and the opposition of his enemies as
the divine judgement upon his sin. The very presence of these
enemies is a source of suffering in the Hymns, not so much because of their personal antagonism as because of their opposition to God. To be with them is like hell on earth (Hymn
6 F). The Community, which excluded such men, was a heaven
on earth. One of the roots of the Community's exclusiveness
was certainly the experience of its earliest members in this
respect. The presence in the Holy Land of gentiles and of
Israelite apostates was an analogous source of suffering on
the national level. It was God's way of punishing Israel for
forsaking the covenant. The covenanters of Qumran were strongly influenced in their thinking here by the "exilic motif"
(the threats of Lev. 26, of Deuteronomy and of the prophets
concerning the coming desolation of the land) and by Daniel's
re-interpretation of this in terms of gentile contamination.
According to Lev. 26, the survivors of the nation in Exile
were to "accept the punishment of their iniquity" by acknow-
ledging the justice of God's judgements upon them. The Community was determined to carry out this programme.

Besides a sense of human weakness and error, the Founder

hymns evince a developing sense of sin and this continues as
an important element in the Community's piety, though in the
later literature there is less sign of it. Even in 1QM the
warriors confess their unworthiness of victory on this account.
For Qumran sin is contagious and contact with sinners is to
be avoided. One of its causes is the activity of evil spirits.

The eschatology of the Community is somewhat confused. They
certainly expected a coming time of wrath. The fire imagery
used to describe this is applied to present sufferings too.
Probably this wrath was to be connected with the holy war
which they expected would start very soon. In 1QS 2:4-9,
4:12-14 the language suggests punishment in the after life,
but it is not clear whether the ultimate destiny of the wicked
is annihilation or eternal punishment. The eternal punishment
of evil spirits is more certain. Ideas of future punishment
are prominent in the Member hymns but absent from the Founder
hymns.

C.   RESULTS OF SALVATION

Salvation includes material benefits. These are mostly
triumph over enemies, long life and everlasting progeny. In
the later period this aspect seems to fill the Community's
vision, in contrast to the earlier stress on "spiritual"
blessings which we find in the Hymns. Closely connected with
the theme of triumph over enemies is the vision of an atonement for the land to be effected by the Community's punitive
role in ridding the country of gentile uncleanness.

The "spiritual" benefits of salvation (a restored relation
with God, knowledge of his counsel, inward joy and peace,
everlasting bliss) together with the response to it (praise,
obedience and service in the Community) are much more prominent in the earlier literature, and especially in the Hymns,
than they are later. There is clear evidence for belief in
eternal life in 1QH and 1QS, although in the former the issue
is often complicated by the use of after-life imagery to describe the life of the Community and its expected vindication.
In CD the focus is rather on the idea of living "to a thousand

generations", a thought which also occurs in 4QpPs37.   There
is no clear reference to belief in a resurrection.

D.   MEANS OF SALVATION

   Salvation is a work of God and manifests his power, love
and justice.   The idea of election is implied in the piety
of the Founder hymns and gains an importance in the Member
hymns which it retains for the remainder of the Community's
history.   The motives for God's saving action are to win
glory for himself, to fulfil his covenant promises and to
satisfy the mysterious goodness of his own nature.   In the
later documents it seems to be implied that he saves also
out of pity for the righteous in their suffering.

   Forgiveness means the acceptance of the person and the end
of wrath towards him.   Sometimes it is spoken of in judicial
terms as a justification or favourable judgement by the King.
Human beings can be the subject of a verb expressing the
divine forgiveness.   The meaning then seems to be that their
actions are a vehicle or a sign of God's forgiveness.   The
language about the messianic atonement in CD 14:8f. means that
the presence and activity of the Messiah will be a sign that
God has forgiven Israel.   Atonement is not merely a synonym
for cleansing or even for forgiveness.   It always carries
overtones of the abolition of the divine wrath.   Sometimes
this is explicitly stated in the context.   Often the verb
"atone" implies the existence of a ground for forgiveness,
but the context does not always answer our question about
what that ground may be.   On two occasions we saw that the
writer was not so much interested in the means of atonement
as in bringing to an end the exilic "desolation" of Israel.[1]

   Forgiveness, though naturally implied in the salvation of
sinful man, is not always mentioned in this connection.   In
the Leader hymns the stress is rather upon instruction as a
means of salvation and this theme is never lost sight of
throughout the history of the Community.   There are two kinds

---

[1]   *Vid. supra*, pp. 11, 103f.

of knowledge which are important for salvation: knowledge of
God's saving ways and knowledge of his will. The former en-
courages the penitent to ask for forgiveness and the latter
enables him to please God in his life. Knowledge enables him
to trust and obey God. Obedience is more greatly stressed
than trust in the Qumran literature. Trust of God is one of
the themes of 1QH, whilst 1QpHab. promises salvation to those
who obey the Law and trust the Teacher of Righteousness. In
the thinking of the Community there could be no effective
obedience to the Law unless there was belief in the Teacher
of Righteousness and his inspired interpretations of it.

One of the reasons for the existence of the Community was to
study the Law and thus prepare the way of the Lord. Knowledge
and trust were intended to issue in obedience, which is seen
as a *sine qua non* for salvation. For the sinner this involves
repentance, for the saint patience. The Community member
accepts the punishment of his sins and knows that in so doing
he is benefiting from the remedial effect that is intended.
There is a corporate aspect to this. The Members constitute
a faithful remnant of Israel, patiently enduring the punishment which God is meting out in accordance with Lev. 26 until
the time decreed both in Leviticus and in Dan. 9 is complete.
The idea of the passage of time as a means of salvation emerges in CD and is maintained in the Herodian period. Earlier,
the present time is seen as the "time of favour", to be followed later by the "day of slaughter" (1QH 15:15-17). The
"favour" was the opportunity to repent, but the later literature shows little interest in this aspect.

The sufferings of the righteous were not viewed as vicarious,
though they were sometimes saving. The Founder's sufferings,
like the pangs of childbirth, brought forth the Community.
The process operated through the truth which he learned by
this experience and passed on to the first Members. Whenever
the sufferings of the Community, or even of the Messiah, were
seen as a prelude to the coming deliverance, this was probably
operative only through the divine pity and vindication.

All this obedience, trust, repentance and patience was

deemed to be the product of a work of God in the human heart.
In the earlier documents this is described in terms of the
gift of a spirit from God, but this way of speaking was not
continued after the Hasmonæan period. This spirit was
sometimes spoken of metaphorically as an atonement.

Discipline is an important means of grace for Qumran. With
the Founder this is God's discipline through the adversities
which he encountered. Later it is the Community's discipline
that is in view, whether administered through reproof or
through penalty. The Community is always seen as a source of
salvation for those who have joined. In the Member hymns the
saving efficacy of the Community is spoken of in terms of the
angels with whom it is united. These constitute a stronghold
for its members.

Atonement rituals were considered to be effective provided
they were rightly carried out and accompanied by a truly
repentant attitude. God cannot be bribed and no wealth can
purchase salvation. When sacrifice is impossible because of
God's judgements upon Israel, piety can be an acceptable
substitute.

In the Founder hymns physical preservation is a means of
salvation. This theme is not continued and in 1QM some of
the Sons of Light are slain in battle. The physical survival
of the Founder was essential so that he could start his work.
Once the Community was in existence attention focuses on
physical preservation for this rather than for the individual
member.

Tho different Hebrew constructions used with the verb "atone"
are probably to be explained in terms of the Old Testament
passages which were consciously or unconsciously alluded to.[1]
These were usually Exod. 32:30, Ezek. 16:63, Ps. 78:38, 79:9,
Dan. 9:24, II Chron. 30:18 and the Day of Atonement laws of
Lev. 16. Most of the passages reflected in this way emphasize
God's forgiveness of Israel in spite of her apostasy. The

---

[1] See the present writer's "Atonement Constructions in the Old Testament
and the Qumran Scrolls", pp. 131-163, also Appendix B *infra*.

constructions most usual in the cultic passages of the priestly literature of the Old Testament are rare at Qumran.

H.H. Rowley's view that the founding of the Community took
place during the Maccabæan crisis[1] and Starcky's theory of
the stages in which the documents were produced would seem
to be compatible with what we have noticed of the development
of the soteriology.

E. CONCLUSION

W.D. Davies has convincingly demonstrated the importance of
the land in the Old Testament scheme of things,[2] and has warn-
ed of the dangers of allowing all the questions we ask of the
Old Testament and of pre-Christian Judaism to be dictated by
the concerns of the New Testament and of Christianity.[3] The
Old Testament and Judaism had their own concerns which are
worthy of study for their own sake as well as being essential
for a complete picture of the background for the New Testament.
Of these, concern for the land was prominent at Qumran.[4] The
present study has attempted to explore the background of some
of the ideas important for Christianity: forgiveness, atonement, salvation. In the process we have been forced to re-
cognise Qumran's concern for the land of Israel, but also the
relationship between this theme and her soteriology: the need
to fulfil Lev. 26 by "accepting the punishment" of exile.

Isa. 53, though meaningful for the New Testament writers,
was something of a puzzle at the time of the Christian movement.[5] In the course of this study the present writer has not
gained the impression that this chapter was the object of
much attention at Qumran. At best there are a few literary
allusions.[6] Instead, many themes, usually associated with
the Suffering Servant to-day, were linked with another pass-

---

[1] *Jewish Apocalyptic and the Dead Sea Scrolls*, London, 1957.

[2] *The Gospel and the Land*, Pt. I.

[3] *Ibid.*, pp. 3-5.

[4] *Ibid.*, pp. 52f.

[5] Acts 8:31, 34.

[6] See Appendix A, *infra*.

age: Lev. 26. This chapter was not a puzzle to the men of
Qumran and its soteriology was demonstrably accepted by them.
Allusions to Lev. 26 can be shown to be much more than literary echoes, they display the covenanters' conscious determination to carry out the programme delineated in that chapter.
In their thinking Lev. 26 formed part of a whole complex of
biblical prediction about the Exile and Restoration, which
we have termed "the exilic motif". The curses of Deuteronomy,
the threats of the prophets and Ezek. 20 are all important
elements here, as well as the re-interpretation of all this
in Daniel, which sees the desolations of Lev. 26 in terms of
gentile pollution.

The verb "atone" seems to be largely used metaphorically.
Often the *modus operandi* is intimated in the context. This
is usually the punishment of the wicked or the work of a
spirit from God. It is never stated to be a vicarious suffering. The overtones of penal substitution, detectable in connection with Old Testament sacrificial atonement, are absent
from the non-cultic atonement passages at Qumran. In the rare
cases where cultic atonement is mentioned, there is no hint
at all about the *modus operandi*. These are the only occasions
when atonement is clearly not metaphorical in this literature.

The general character of the Community's soteriology was
such that there was little likelihood of ideas of supererogatory suffering or of a pool of merits finding a place in their
thinking. In early stages the stress on human unworthiness
was too great. In the later stages when there might have been
an openness for the conception of merit (though we found no
evidence that the concept had actually entered their theology)
there was no longer enough interest in outsiders even to be
concerned with those who might join the Community later.

Returning to the question with which this study opened, we
may now say that our first-hand source for the sectarian Judaism of the time of Christ does not seem to provide a background
for the way the gospels have presented the significance of the
sufferings of Jesus. One of three consequences would seem to
follow.

i.   Since the gospels' presentation of the thinking of Jesus
is out of context with what is now known about his probable
thought background in sectarian Judaism, this presentation is
to be understood as a reflection of the thinking of the early
church.

ii. The background of the thinking of Jesus is to be found
in Rabbinical and Hellenistic Judaism at this point, in the
belief in the atoning value of the death of the martyrs.[1]

iii. The thinking of Jesus on the atoning value of suffering
and death represents his own original interpretation of the
fourth Servant Song.   It was not mediated to him through con-
temporary Judaism.[2]

---

[1] E.g. Jeremias, *New Testament Theology*, pp. 287f.   J. Roloff, however,
has cautioned that the evidence is weak for such a belief before A.D. 50:
"Anfänge der soteriologischen Deutung des Todes Jesu (Mk. X. 45 und Lk.
XXII. 27)," *NTS*, 19 (1972), pp. 46-48.

[2] Cf. Dodd, *According to the Scriptures*, London, 1952, pp. 110, 123f.

APPENDIX A

PUTATIVE ALLUSIONS TO THE ISAIANIC SERVANT

Many of the points raised in favour of a Servant role at
Qumran[1] have been answered in detail by Carmignac.[2] The
assumptions behind some of the arguments have been refuted
by Holm-Nielsen[3] and Jeremias.[4] Since the present study has
not discovered any striking Servant motifs in the Scrolls,
those passages which have not been scrutinized in Carmignac's
article should be examined as well as the larger principles
of interpretation involved.

Brownlee sees a reference to Isa. 42:1 in 1QH 7:6f.,[5] but
"uphold" is not the same word in the Hebrew and the very common word "spirit" turns out to be the only piece of vocabulary
shared by the two passages. He sees allusions to the same
text in 1QH 13:18f., 14:25 and 17:26.[6] The first has the
words "servant", "spirit" and "give" in common with the Isaiah
verse, the second only "servant" and "spirit" and the third
"servant". "spirit" and "upon". If all three had the identical formula of the Isaiah passage, we would be impressed, even
though each individual word is very common indeed. Brownlee
admits that the use of the phrase "thy servant" in the hymns
cannot be pressed as a Servant allusion, since it could be
explained as a term of humble address to God, but he argues
that whenever the spirit is mentioned in connection with this
phrase an allusion already exists. He adduces these passages
as examples. This defence is rather weakened, however, by the
point made by Carmignac that "thy servant" never occurs in the

---

[1] *Vid. supra*, p. 2 nn. 2-5.

[2] *Rev. Qum.*, 2 (June, 1960), pp. 357-394.

[3] *Hodayot*, pp. 301ff.

[4] *TDNT* V, p. 687 n. 20.

[5] *NTS*, 3 (1956/7), p. 20.

[6] *Ibid.*

whole of Isaiah, though it is frequent in the Psalms,[1] and
the point made by Jeremias that the phrase is never applied
to the Founder in the third person and is never combined with
references to the Servant Songs.[2]

Some of the 1QH parallels adduced are simply a matter of
similar contents. There is no verbal resemblance.[3] Three
only of the Servant allusions adduced for 1QH are certain:
7:7-10 (cf. Isa. 50:4-9), 8:35f. (cf. Isa. 50:4) and 18:14
(cf. Isa. 61:1-3).[4]

Brownlee has claimed Servant allusions in 1QS too.[5] 4:18ff.
contains one or two literary echoes of the fourth Servant
Song, but they are very faint and other Old Testament material
is reflected in the passage besides.[6] There is no evidence
that the purification here is by means of suffering. The
method of purification is explicitly stated to be the action
of a spirit from God and the learning of the truth. The
present writer has already commented on the allusion of 8:4ff.[7]

Commentators often link the Servant figure with the *maskîlîm*
of the book of Daniel. Since Daniel was clearly applying the
Servant ideal to the faithful of the Maccabaean crisis (the
maskîlîm) and since the Qumran covenanters were the lineal
descendants of these Chasidim, it might be argued that it is
not unreasonable to suppose that they continued the exegetical
tradition of Daniel.[8] The following points should be borne in
mind, however.

---

[1]   *Rev. Qum.*, 7, p. 385.

[2]   *Loc. cit.*

[3]   E.g. Dupont-Sommer, *Le Livre des Hymnes*, pp. 17f. on 1QH 8:7 (cf. Isa.
49:2, 50:7), 1QH 9:10, 24-26 (cf. Isa. 53:7); Brownlee, *The Meaning of the
Qumran Scrolls for the Bible*, p. 141 on 1QH 9:29-32 (cf. Isa. 53:2).

[4]   See Holm-Nielsen, *op. cit.*, *ad loc.* and Jeremias, *loc. cit.*

[5]   4:18ff., 8:4ff. see *The United Presbyterian*, 111 (30.11. '53 - 28.12.
'53) and *BASOR*, no. 135 (Oct., 1954), pp. 33ff.

[6]   4:20 reflects the language of Mal. 3:3 as closely as that of Isa. 52:4,
if not more so. See Wernberg-Møller, *op. cit.*, pp. 85f. n. 70.

[7]   *Supra*, pp. 66f.

[8]   Cf. e.g. Bruce, *New Testament Development*, pp. 90ff., *Biblical Exegesis*,
pp. 55, 58f; Brownlee, *BASOR*, no. 132 (Dec., 1953), pp. 12ff.

i.   Daniel was written secretly (Dan. 12:9), rather than as
a community effort of the Chasidim.   The identification of the
latter with the Servant of the fourth Song may have been the
private insight of the author and not noticed by the first
readers.

ii.   The Essenes broke away from the Chasidim and one of the
points of controversy was the interpretation of prophecy.[1]

iii. We cannot be sure that even the author of Daniel regarded
all the Servant Songs as an entity, though he clearly thought
of the fourth Song as such, since he alludes to the beginning
and the end of it in the vocabulary he uses.[2]   How much less
certain can we be that a "Servant figure" existed as a prophetic entity for the Chasidim or for Qumran!   Bruce character-
izes the exegesis of the latter as atomistic.[3]

---

[1]   1QH 5:25, *vid. supra*, p. 8, pp. 14-16.

[2]   *Vid. supra*, p. 41 n. 5.

[3]   *Biblical Exegesis*, p. 16.

APPENDIX B

כפר USAGE IN THE OLD TESTAMENT AND THE SCROLLS

Recent literature disagrees about whether כפר means basically
propitiation (appeasement)[1] or expiation (cleansing).[2] In
1974[3] I argued that the usage as it developed in the Old Testament and the Scrolls had a double origin:-
(a) A Hebrew social usage: appease.
(b) An Assyrian cultic usage: cleanse.
As a result, the subsequent development allowed for a double
denotation of the verb, according to its subject:-
(1) When man is the subject, it means to perform some action
whereby the divine forgiveness is procured.
(2) When God is the subject, it means to forgive.
Usage (1) is always spiritualized to the extent that God is
never the direct object of the verb. Man does not "appease"
God. The connotation of the verb remained constant, however.
It always had overtones of the putting away of wrath.

The study analysed the usage of the root כפר throughout
the Old Testament and the Scrolls and attempted to account
for the various constructions which emerged. For the detailed
discussion, the reader should consult the article itself, but
I am reproducing here the tabulated conclusions and the data
so that he can pick out the various usages referred to in the
course of the present monograph and see how extensive and
influential they were and the nature of the evidence for each.
For convenience of presentation here, I shall start with the
tabulated conclusions and present the data later.

A. CLASSIFICATION OF כפר USAGES

Apart from the material usage (daub, bitumen, henna) we may

---

[1] Morris, *op. cit.*

[2] Lyonnet, in *Analecta Biblica*, 48, *Sin, Redemption and Sacrifice*, Rome,
1970, pp. 127-136.

[3] "Atonement Constructions", *The Evangelical Quarterly*, 46, pp. 131-163.

distinguish four main usages of כפר in the Old Testament and
three at Qumran: the social, the socio-religious, the prophetic, the Levitical, the Qumranian, the Serek usage and the
Damascus usage. Within some of these there are various sub-
usages, some of them very important (e.g. the Isaianic within
the prophetic usage). The following table sets out all the
more important types and sub-types.

The letters in the second column represent putative sources
of the Hexateuch, but the letters in the last column refer
back to the usage symbols in the first.

	Usage	Main Instances	Subject	Object	Origin
A	social	Gen. 32:21 Prov. 16:14	offender	face *or* wrath of offended	early
B	social (*kopher*)	throughout O.T.	offender	himself, his "soul"	early
C	socio-religious	II Sam. 21:3	offender's represent-ative		A
D	Mosaic	Exod. 32:30 4Q Dib. Ham. 2:9	offender's represent-ative	בעד offence	C, entreaty language
E	soc.-rel. (*kopher*)	throughout, except Assyrian	man	his brother, his "soul"	B
F	Isaianic	Isa., D, Pss., Qumran	usually God	ל person, dir. obj.=sin	prophetism, Assyrian
G	soc.-rel. Isaianic	Isa. 43:3 1Q 34 1:5f.	God	the elect (*kopher*)	E, F
H	Jeremiah's	Jer. 18:23 Ps. 79:9	God	על sin	prophetism, Levitical
I	Levitical	H, P, Chron-icler, Ezekiel, Qumran	usually priests, means, financer	על persons, על or מן sins; never dir. obj.=person or sin	spiritualized A
J	Levitical territorial	Num. 35:33 Ezek. 16:63		ל territory, ל sin	
K	Levitical Assyrian	P, Ezekiel	priests	dir. obj.= sacred objects	Assyrian

Usage	Main Instances	Subject	Object	Origin
L Levitical solemn	Lev. 9:7; 16 Ezek. 45:17 1QM 2:5	as in I	בעד people	I, D
M Danielic	Dan. 9:24	period of time	dir. obj.= iniquity	F. Lev. 26
N Qumranian	1QH 17:12 1QS 11:14 CD 3:18	God	בעד iniquity	D re-interpreted by Exod. 34:6f.
O Serek	1QS, 1QSa	Community	בעד land	J, L, Community's view of its role
P Damascus	CD	God	בעד repentant	II Chron. 30:18 (a rare form of Levitical)

We shall now set out in tabular form how the presence of these particular usages was detected in the material studied.

In the tables which follow, column 1 will give the reference in the English Bible, followed by the Hebrew reference whenever this differs. Other words and abbreviations in brackets indicate the putative source when necessary.

Column 2 gives the subject of the verb כפר. It should be noted that when the verb is in the infinitive it is sometimes difficult to see what subject is in the author's mind, if any.

Column 3 shows the conjugation of the verb and also indicates if it is in the infinitive.

Column 4 gives the person or object towards which the action of the verb is directed, preceded by the preposition or construction which governs it.

Column 5 indicates the expression for the sin which is said to be atoned for, preceded by the preposition or construction governing it.

Column 6 shows the means by which the action of the verb is attained, preceded by the preposition governing the means.

If the verb is in the passive, the agent is given in column 2 and the subject, which is invariably sin, in column 5.

These are equivalent to the subject and direct object respectively of the active construction. If the verb is used absolutely, this is shown in columns 4 and 5.

If the noun *kopher* is used, this is indicated in column 3,
whilst the person giving the *kopher* is shown in column 2, the
person for whom it is given in column 4, any offence involved
in column 5 and the nature of the *kopher* in column 6.

Wherever there is doubt about the subject, the object or
the means of the action of the verb, this is shown by means of
brackets.

The letters preceding each reference in column 1 represent
the usage which I judge to be operative in each case. Letters
elsewhere represent the putative source.

B. THE EARLY LITERATURE

	1	2	3	4	5	6
C	II Sam. 21:3 (Early S.)	David	pi'el	absolutely		כ what?
A	Gen. 32:20 (21) (J)	Jacob	pi'el	Dir. obj. Esau's face		כ gift
D	Exod. 32:30 (E)	Moses	pi'el		בעד your sin	(inter-cession)
B	Exod. 21:30 (E)	man	*kopher*	פדין נפשו	(homicide)	(money)

C. THE ASSYRIAN PERIOD

	1	2	3	4	5	6
	I Sam. 3:14 (Late S.)		hithpa'el negative		iniquity of Eli's house	כ sacrifices
B	I Sam. 12:3 (Late s.)	guilty	*kopher*	guilty		bribe
B	Amos 5:12	oppressors	*kopher*	oppressors		bribe
F	Isa. 6:7	seraph	pu'al		thy sin	coal from altar
F	Isa. 22:14	(God)	pu'al negative	ל you (Judah)	this iniquity	

APPENDIX B: כפר USAGE

	1	2	3	4	5	6
F	Isa. 28:18		pu'al negative		Judah's covenant with death	
F	Deut. 21:8 (D) - a	God	pi'el	ל thy people		(heifer ritual)
F	Deut. 21:8 (D) - b	(God)	nithpa'el	ל them	the shed blood	(doing right)

The hithpa'el in I Sam. 3:14 could be taken as the reflexive
of the pi'el in the original sense of "appease". Even if it
has the force of a passive, God cannot be the logical subject,
since sacrifices are mentioned as the means of atonement.
"Iniquity", which is clearly the logical object of the action
of the verb, probably means "punishment" and is almost a per-
sonification, as the agent of wrath. In this way there is a
link with the social usage. Yet the sentence could easily be
rendered, "The iniquity of Eli's house shall not be purged by
sacrifices", which is very similar to the Isaianic usage. This
passage could form a bridge between the social and the Isaianic
usages.

D. JEREMIAH AND THE EXILIC PERIOD

	1	2	3	4	5	6
H	Jer. 18:23	God	pi'el negative		על their iniquity	
I	Lev. 17:11 (H)	blood	pi'el inf.	על your souls		
I	"	blood	pi'el		absolutely	ב the soul
I	Lev. 19:22 (H)	priest	pi'el	על offerer	על his sin	ב ram of guilt offer- ing
I	Lev. 23:28 (H)		pi'el inf.	על you		(Day of Atonement)
J	Ezek. 16:63	God	pi'el	ל Jerusalem	ל all thou hast done	(everlasting covenant)
K	Ezek. 43:20	Ezek. via Zadokites	pi'el	dir. obj. settle		(blood)

	1	2	3	4	5	6
K	Ezek. 43:26	Zadokites	pi'el	את altar		
I	Ezek. 45:15	(people)	pi'el inf.	על prince		offerings
L	Ezek. 45:17	(prince)	pi'el inf.	בעד house of Israel		offerings
K	Ezek. 45:20	ye, via priest	pi'el	את house of God		blood
	Deut. 32:43 (Song of Moses)	God	pi'el	dir. obj. his land, his people		(taking vengeance on enemies)
G	Isa. 43:3	God	*kopher*	Israel		Egypt
	Isa. 47:11	Babylon	pi'el negative		disaster	(magic)
F	Isa. 27:9 (Isa. Apoc.)		pu'al		iniquity	ב destruction of idol altars

Isa. 47:11 seems to be a peculiar combination of the Isaianic and the social usages, disaster being pictured as an evil spirit which cannot be appeased, or as a stain which cannot be wiped away.

The strange construction in Deut. 32:43 yields the renderings "ransom", "cleanse" or "forgive". Since the context mentions the destruction of Israel's enemies in close connection with her deliverance, there is perhaps an echo of the socio-religious usage with *kopher*: God gives the wicked as the ransom payment for his people.[1]

E. THE PRIESTLY CODE ("P")

The usual expression in P with כפר is given as the first item in the list which follows. There are about thirty instances of this, though not every term in the formula is expressed in every instance. Sometimes כפר is used absolutely in a way that is quite compatible with this formula, including Exod. 29:33, where it is used absolutely in the passive.

---

[1] See also Prov. 21:18, *infra*, p. 133.

	1	2	3	4	5	6
I	usually	priests, Moses, Aaron	pi'el	על persons	מן sins	ב offering
	Gen. 6:14	Noah	qal	ark (dir. obj.)		ב pitch (*kopher*)
	Exod. 29:36	Moses	pi'el	על altar		(sacrifices)
	Exod. 29:37	Moses	pi'el	על altar		(sacrifices)
	Exod. 30:10 *bis*	Aaron	pi'el	על horns of altar		מן blood
I	Exod. 30:15	Israel	pi'el inf.	על your souls		(half shekel)
I	Exod. 30:16	half shekel	pi'el inf.	על your souls		(half shekel
I	Lev. 1:4	burnt offering	pi'el inf.	על offerer		(burnt offering)
I	Lev. 4:35, 5:13	priest	pi'el	על offerer	על his sin	(sin offerings)
I	Lev. 5:18	priest	pi'el	על offerer	על his ignorance	(ram of guilt offering)
I	Lev. 6:30 (23)	blood	pi'el inf.	absolutely		(sin offering)
	Lev. 8:15	Moses	pi'el	על altar		
L	Lev. 9:7	Aaron	pi'el	בעד the people and himself		(burnt and sin offerings)
I	Lev. 10:17	flesh of sin offering	pi'el	על congregation		(eating flesh of sin offering)
	Lev. 14:53	priest	pi'el	על leprous house		(living bird)
	Lev. 16:10	Aaron	pi'el inf.	absolutely		על living goat
	Lev. 16:16	Aaron	pi'el	על sanctuary	מן sins of Israel	(blood within veil)
L	Lev. 16:17	Aaron	pi'el	בעד himself, his house, the congregation)		(sprinkled blood)

	1	2	3	4	5	6
	Lev. 16:18	Aaron	pi'el	על altar		(blood)
K	Lev. 16:20	Aaron	pi'el	את holy places, altar		(blood)
L	Lev. 16:24	Aaron	pi'el	בעד himself, the people		(burnt offerings)
K	Lev. 16:33	priest	pi'el	את holy places, altar		(Day of Atonement rituals)
	Num. 8:19	Levites	pi'el inf.	על Israel- ites		(Levites)
I	Num. 16:46f. (17:11f.)	Aaron	pi'el	על the people		(incense offering
	Num. 25:13	Phinehas	pi'el	על Israel- ites		(punishing the guilty)
I	Num. 31:50	Israel	pi'el inf.	על their souls		(spoil)
J	Num. 35:33	(Israel)	pu'al negative	ל the land	ל blood shed	ב blood of killer
E	Exod. 30:12	Israelite	*kopher*	his soul		(money)
E	Num. 35:31f.	(guilty)	*kopher* negative	soul of killer		

The preposition על can be used to govern the sacred or
other objects to be atoned for (Exod. 29:37, Lev. 8:15, 14:53,
16:16, 18), but sometimes it has a local force, "upon" (Exod.
29:36). In Exod. 30:10 the sense seems to be that Aaron is
to make atonement <u>upon</u> the horns of the altar of incense once
a year, thus making atonement <u>for</u> this altar. In Lev. 16:10
the preposition על governing the means of atonement (the living goat) reflects the fact that Israel's sins were laid <u>upon</u>
it.

In Num. 8:19 כפר means to act as a substitute. It cannot
mean to perform sacrificial atonement, since this was the pre-
rogative of the priests.

In Num. 25:13 Phinehas atoned for Israel (averted the divine wrath) by punishing the guilty in her midst.

Gen. 6:14 is the only instance of the qal, meaning to daub. It may be termed the material usage. Similarly the noun *kopher*, in the same verse, means bitumen.

F. THE POST-EXILIC PERIOD

	1	2	3	4	5	6
I	I Chron. 6:49 (34)	Aaron, his sons	pi'el inf.	על Israel		(activity of subject
I	II Chron. 29:34	priests	pi'el inf.	על all Israel		(Hezekiah's sacrifice
	II Chron. 30:18	good Yahweh	pi'el	בעד every-one who prepares his heart		(Hezekiah's prayer)
I	Neh. 10:33 (34)	the people	pi'el inf.	על Israel		(sin offerings)
M	Dan. 9:24	seventy weeks	pi'el inf.		dir. obj. iniquity	(seventy weeks)

II Chron. 30:18 is a special form of the Levitical usage. Exceptionally, God is the subject, because there was no provision under the Levitical system for the grossly incorrect condition of the worshippers. The preposition בעד adds a note of special solemnity.

G. THE POETIC BOOKS

	1	2	3	4	5	6
E	Ps. 49:7 (8)	a man	*kopher* negative	his brother		
F	Ps. 65:3 (4)	God	pi'el		dir. obj. our transgressions	
F	Ps. 78:38	God	pi'el	(Israel)	dir. obj. their iniquity	
H	Ps. 79:9	God	pi'el		על our sins	

		1	2	3	4	5	6
B	Prov. 6:35	adulterer	*kopher* negative	himself	adultery	gifts
B	Prov. 13:8	a man	*kopher*	his soul		riches
F	Prov. 16:6	(the repentant)	pu'al		iniquity	ב mercy and truth
A	Prov. 16:14	a wise man	pi'el	the king's wrath		
E	Prov. 21:18		*kopher*	the righteous		the wicked
E	Job 33:24	angel	*kopher*	(man threatened by death)		
E	Job 36:18	(Job)	*kopher* negative	(Job)		(money)

H. THE EMERGING QUMRAN COMMUNITY

		1	2	3	4	5	6
D	4Q Dib. Ham. 2:9	Moses	pi'el		בעד their sin	(intercession)
F	1QH 4:37	God	pi'el		dir. obj. iniquity	(ב thy צדקה)
E	1QH 15:24		*kopher* negative		works of evil	
N	1QH 17:12	(God)	pi'el inf.		(בעד)	
F	1QH f.2:13		pi'el inf.		dir. obj. guilt	(spirit of holiness)

15:24 states that God will not accept a *kopher* for evil
deeds. Riches will not avail for acceptance before God.
Here we are in the sphere of the socio-religious use of the
term *kopher*, with which we have become familiar from the Old
Testament. The use of ל governing the sins after the noun
kopher is not found in the Old Testament. It is, however,
found after the verb כפר in Num. 35:33, in close connection
with the *kopher* idea, as the context shows.

I. THE MANUAL OF DISCIPLINE AND THE MESSIANIC RULE

	1	2	3	4	5	6
F	1QS 2:8	God	pi'el inf. negative		dir. obj. your iniquity	
F	1QS 3:6		pu'al		man's ways all his iniquities	ב the spirit of the counsel of the truth of God
F	1QS 3:8		pu'al		his sin	ב upright and humble spirit
F	1QS 5:6	(God)	pi'el inf.	ל all who volunteer		
O	1QS 8:6	formed community	pi'el inf.	בעד the land		
O	1QS 8:10	formed community	pi'el inf.	בעד the land		
H	1QS 9:4	Community as foundation	pi'el inf.		על guilt of transgression	(spirit of holiness, discipline)
N	1QS 11:14	God	pi'el		בעד all my iniquity	ב his great goodness
O	1QSa 1:3	Community	pi'el inf.	בעד] the la]nd		

J. THE DAMASCUS DOCUMENT

	1	2	3	4	5	6
P	CD 2:5	God/his goodness	pi'el inf.	בעד the repentant		(God's kindness)
N	CD 3:18	God	pi'el		בעד their iniquity	ב his wonderful mysteries
P	CD 4:6	God	pi'el	בעד first members		
H	CD 4:9	God	pi'el inf.		על their sins (of first members)	

	1	2	3	4	5	6
P	CD 4:9	God	pi'el	בעד later members		
M	CD 14:19	(Messiah)	pi'el		dir. obj. their in-iquity	
P	CD 20:34	God	pi'el	בעד those who fulfil Community programme		(trusting in God's name)

K. OTHER QUMRAN MATERIAL

	1	2	3	4	5	6
L	1QM 2:5	priests	pi'el inf.	בעד God's congregation		(offerings)
G	1Q34 1:5f.	God	*kopher*	the elect		the wicked
I	11Q Melch 7f.		pi'el inf.	על all the sons . . .		ב + ?
I	1Q Myst f. 6:2		pi'el		על ignor-ance	
I	1Q Myst f. 6:3		pi'el inf.	dir. obj. + ?		
I	1Q DM 3:11		pu'al		absolutely	(Day of Atonement rites)
F	1Q DM 4:3		pu'al	ל them		ב it (? shed blood)
	4Q Ord 2:2		pi'el inf.		ל your sins	

BIBLIOGRAPHY

Allegro, John M., *The People of the Dead Sea Scrolls*, New York, 1958.

Baillet, Maurice, "Un recueil liturgique de Qumrân, grotte 4: 'Les paroles des luminaires'," *Rev. Bib.*, 68 (1961), pp. 195-250.

Becker, Jürgen, *Das Heil Gottes*, Göttingen, 1964.

Black, Matthew, *The Dead Sea Scrolls and Christian Doctrine*, London, 1966.

Black, Matthew, *The Scrolls and Christian Origins*, New York, 1961.

Bouquet, A.C., *Sacred Books of the World*, London, 1954.

Braun, H., "Römmer 7,7-25 und das Selbstverständnis des Qumran-Frommen," *Z. Theo. K.*, 56 (1959), pp. 1-18.

Brownlee, W.H., "Anthropoloqy and Soteriology in the Dead Sea Scrolls and in the New Testament," in *The Use of the Old Testament in the New and Other Essays*, ed. James M. Efird, Durham, N.C., 1972, pp. 210-240.

Brownlee, W.H., "The Cross of Christ in the Light of Ancient Scrolls," *The United Presbyterian*, Pittsburg, 111:48-51 (30.11'53 - 28.12.'53).

Brownlee, W.H., *The Dead Sea Manual of Discipline, Translation and Notes*, New Haven, Conn., 1951.

Brownlee, W.H., *The Meaning of the Qumran Scrolls for the Bible*, New York, 1964.

Brownlee, W.H., "Messianic Motifs of Qumran and the New Testament," *NTS*, 3 (1956/7), pp. 12-30.

Brownlee, W.H., "The Servant of the Lord in the Qumran Scrolls," *BASOR*, 132 (Dec., 1953), pp. 8-15 and 135 (Oct., 1954), pp. 33-38.

Bruce, F.F., *Biblical Exegesis in the Qumran Texts*, Grand Rapids, 1959.

Bruce, F.F., *New Testament Development of Old Testament Themes*, Grand Rapids, c. 1968.

Brunner, Emil, *The Christian Doctrine of Creation and Redemption, Dogmatics*, II, tr. by O. Wyon, London, 1952.

Burchard, C., "Bibliographie zu den Handschriften vom Toten Meer," *BZAW*, 76 (1957) and 89 (1965).

Burrows, Millar, *The Dead Sea Scrolls*, New York, 1955.

Burrows, Millar; Trever, John C.; Brownlee, William H. edd., *The Dead Sea Scrolls of St. Mark's Monastery*, vol. II, fasc. 2, New Haven, Conn., 1951.

Carmignac, J., "Les citations de l'Ancien Testament, et spécialement des Poèmes du Serviteur, dans les *Hymnes* de Qumrân," *Rev. Qum.*, 2 (1959/60), pp. 357-394.

Carmignac, J., "Le document de Qumrân sur Melkisédeq," *Rev. Qum.*, 7 (1970), pp. 343-378.

Carmignac, J., "La notion d'eschatologie dans la Bible et à Qumrân," *Rev. Qum.*, 7 (1969), pp. 17-31.

Carmignac, J., *Les textes de Qumrân*, Paris, 1961.

Carmignac, J., "La théologie de la souffrance dans les Hymnes de Qumrân," *Rev. Qum.*, 3 (1961/2), pp. 365-386.

Chamberlain, John V., "Toward a Qumran Soteriology," *Novum Testamentum*, 3 (1959), pp. 305-313.

Charles, R.H., *Apocrypha and Pseudepigrapha of the Old Testament*, 2 vols., London, 1913.

Coote, Robert B., "'MW‹D HT‹NYT' in 4Q 171 (pesher Psalm 37), fragments 1-2, col II, line 9," *Rev. Qum.*, 8 (1972), pp. 81-85.

Crowfoot, G.M., "The Linen Textiles," *Discoveries in the Judæan Desert*, I, pp. 18-38.

Davies, W.D., *The Gospel and the Land*, Berkeley, c. 1974.

Delcor, M., *Les hymnes de Qumran (Hodayot)*, Paris, 1962.

Discoveries in the Judæan Desert, Oxford,
    Vol. I, Barthélemy, D. and Milik, J.T., 1955.
    Vol. III, Baillet M., Milik, J.T. and de Vaux, R., 1962.
    Vol. V, Allegro, John M., 1968.

Dodd, C.H., *According to the Scriptures*, London, 1952.

Dodd, C.H., *The Epistle of Paul to the Romans*, London, 1932.

Dombrowski, B.W., "יחד in 1QS and τὸ κοινόν," *Harvard Theological Review*, 59 (1966), pp. 293-307.

Dombrowski, B.W., "The Idea of God in 1Q Serek," *Rev. Qum.*, 7 (1971), pp. 515-531.

Driver, G.R., *The Judæan Scrolls*, New York, 1965.

Dupont-Sommer, A., *The Essene Writings from Qumran*, tr. by G. Vermes, Oxford, 1961.

Dupont-Sommer, A., "La 'Règle' de la Communauté de la Nouvelle Alliance," *Revue de l'histoire des religions*, 138 (1950), pp. 5-21.

Flusser, D., "Pharisees, Sadducees and Essenes in Pesher Nahum," (Eng. summary) *Immanuel*, 1 (1972), pp. 39-41.

Garnet, P., "Atonement Constructions in the Old Testament and the Qumran Scrolls," *The Evangelical Quarterly*, 46 (1974), pp. 131-163.

Gärtner, B., *The Temple and the Community in Qumran and the New Testament*, Cambridge, 1965.

Glasson, T.F., *Greek Influence in Jewish Eschatology*, London, 1961.

Grelot, Pierre (review of *Le Targum de Job de la Grotte XI de Qumrân*, edd. J.P.M. van der Ploeg and A.S. van der Woude), *Rev. Qum.*, 8 (1972), pp. 105-114.

Grundmann, W., "The Teacher of Righteousness of Qumran and the Question of Justification by Faith in the Theology of the Apostle Paul," in *Paul and Qumran*, ed. J. Murphy-O'Connor, London, 1968, pp. 85-114.

Habermann, A.M., *Megilloth Midbar Yehuda*, Israel, 1959.

Holm-Nielsen, Svend, *Hodayot, Psalms from Qumran*, Aarus, 1960.

Iwry, Samuel, "A New Designation for the Luminaries in Ben Sira and in the Manual of Discipline (1QS)," *BASOR*, 200 (1970), pp. 41-47.

Jaubert, A., *La notion d'alliance dans le Judaïsme aux abords de l'ère chrétienne*, Paris, c. 1963.

Jaubert, A., "Le Pays de Damas," *Rev. Bib.*, 65 (1958), pp. 214-248.

Jeremias, Joachim, *New Testament Theology: the Proclamation of Jesus*, New York, 1971.

Jeremias, Joachim, παῖς θεοῦ, *TDNT* V.

Johnston, George, "'Spirit' and 'Holy Spirit' in the Qumran Literature," *New Testament Sidelights*, essays in honour of Alexander Converse Purdy, ed. by H.K. McArthur, Hartford, 1960.

Jongeling, B., *Le Rouleau de la Guerre*, Assen, 1962.

Kuhn, K.G., *Konkordanz zu den Qumrantexten*, Göttingen, 1960.

Kuhn, K.G., "Nachträge zur 'Konkordanz zu den Qumrantexten'," *Rev. Qum.*, 4 (May, 1963), כפר and cognates p. 202.

Lambert, G., *Le Manuel de Discipline du désert de Juda*, Louvain, 1951.

Leaney, A.R.C., *The Rule of Qumran and its Meaning*, London, 1966.

Le Déault, R., "Une citation de *Lévitique* 26,45 dans le *Document de Damas* I,4; VI,2," *Rev. Qum.*, 6 (1967/8), pp. 289-291.

Lisowsky, G., *Konkordanz zum hebräischen alten Testament*, Stuttgart, 1958.

Lohse, Eduard, *Die Texte aus Qumran*, Darmstadt, 1964.

Lyonnet, S., "De notione expiationis," *Verbum Domini*, Rome, 37 (1959), pp. 336-352, 38 (1960), pp. 65-75.

Lyonnet, S., *De peccato et redemptione, II: de vocabulario redemptionis*, Rome, 1960, pp. 66-117.

Lyonnet, S., "Justification, jugement, rédemption, principalement dans l'épître aux Romains," *Littérature et théologie pauliniennes*, Bruges, 1960.

Lyonnet, S. and Sabourin, L., *Sin, Redemption and Sacrifice*, Rome, 1970.

Mansoor, Menahem, *The Dead Sea Scrolls*, Grand Rapids, 1964.

Mansoor, Menahem, *The Thanksgiving Hymns*, Grand Rapids, 1961.

Milik, J.T., *Ten Years of Discovery in the Wilderness of Judœa*, Naperville, Illinois, 1958.

Moroney, M.J., *Facts from Figures*, 2nd. ed., London, 1953.

Morris, Leon, *The Apostolic Preaching of the Cross*, London, 1955.

Mowinkel, S., *The Psalms in Israel's Worship*, tr. by D.R. Ap-Thomas, vol. II, Oxford, 1962.

Mowry, Lucetta, *The Dead Sea Scrolls and the Early Church*, Chicago, 1962.

Nicholls, William, "Liberation as a Religious Theme," *CJT*, 16 (1970), pp. 140-154.

Ploeg, J. van der, *Le rouleau de la guerre*, Leiden, 1959.

Ploeg, J. van der and Woude, A.S. van der, *Le Targum de Job de la Grotte XI de Qumran*, Leiden, 1971.

Rabin, C., *Qumran Studies*, London, 1957.

Rabin, C., *The Zadokite Documents*, Oxford, 1954.

Rad, G. von, *Old Testament Theology*, tr. by D.M.G. Stalker, Edinburgh, vol. I, 1962; vol. II, 1966.

Reventlow, H. Graf von, *Rechtfertigung im Horizont des Alten Testaments*, Munich, 1971.

Ringgren, H., *The Faith of Qumran*, tr. by Emile T. Sander, Philadelphia, c. 1963.

Roloff, J., "Anfänge der soteriologische Deutung des Todes Jesu (Mk. X.45 und Lk. XXII.27)," *NTS*, 19 (1972), pp. 38-64.

Rowley, H.H., *Jewish Apocalyptic and the Dead Sea Scrolls*, London, 1957.

Sanders, J.A., *The Dead Sea Psalms Scroll*, Ithaca, N.Y., 1967.

Schmidt, H.H., "Schöpfung, Gerechtigkeit und Heil. 'Schöpfungstheologie' als Gesamthorizont biblischer Theologie," *Z. Theo. K.*, 70 (1973), pp. 1-19.

Schrenk, G., ἐκδικέω, *TDNT* II, pp. 442-446.

Schulz, S., "Zur Rechtfertigung aus Gnaden in Qumran und bei Paulus,"
   Z. Theo. K., 56 (1959), pp. 155-185.

Starcky, J., "Les quatre étapes du messianisme à Qumran," *Rev. Bib.*,
   70 (1963), pp. 481-505.

Stuhlmacher, P., *Gerechtigkeit Gottes bei Paulus*, Göttingen, 1965.

Sukenik, E.L. ed., *The Dead Sea Scrolls of the Hebrew University*, Jerusalem, 1955.

Talmon, S., "The Sectarian יחד," *Vetus Testamentum*, 3 (1953), pp. 130-140.

Thiering, Barbara, "Suffering and Asceticism at Qumran, as Illustrated
   in the Hodayot," *Rev. Qum.*, 8 (1974), p. 405.

Trever, John C. ed., *Scrolls from Qumran Cave I*, Jerusalem, 1972.

Trever, J.C., "1Q Dan^a, the Latest of the Qumran Manuscripts," *Rev. Qum.*,
   7 (Apr., 1970), pp. 277-286.

Vaux, Roland de, *L'archéologie et les manuscrits de la mer Morte*, London,
   1961.

Vermes, G., *The Dead Sea Scrolls in English*, London, 1965.

Vriezen, Th. C., *The Religion of Ancient Israel*, tr. by Hubert Hoskins,
   London, 1967.

Wallenstein, M., *The Nezer and the Submission in Suffering Hymn from the
   Dead Sea Scrolls*, Istanbul, 1957.

Wernberg-Møller, P., *The Manual of Discipline*, Leiden, 1957.
   - reviewed by J.T. Milik in *Rev. Bib.*, 67 (1960), pp. 410-416, giving
   a list of the variant readings of Serek fragments from Caves 4 and 5.

Yadin, Yigael, *The Scroll of the War of the Sons of Light against the
   Sons of Darkness*, tr. by B. and C. Rabin, London, 1962.

INDEX OF PASSAGES

INDEX OF SUBJECTS

Relationship with God, see Communion
Remedial punishment 9n, 10f, 17ff, 27ff, 32ff, 39, 46f, 50f, 116
Renewal of creation 46f, 48
Repentance 10n, 22ff, 32ff, 49, 51f, 54, 60, 89, 97f, 110f, 116
Reproof 42n, 42f, 51f, (63), 64f, 94f, 95n, 116f
Responsibility, corporate, see Corporate
individual, see Individual
Restoration of Israel, see Return
Resurrection 22ff, 35, 46f, 49, 93n, 114f
Return from Exile 10f, 27ff, 29n, 35, 63f, 79, 88, 101f, 103, 105, 109f, 115, 119
Righteousness 46f, 57, 87f
God's 9, 43n, 45, 46f, 73-80, 83n, 100n, 112ff
man's 42n, 46f, 48, 75n, 76f, 80, 91f, 100, 105, 107
punitive 43n, 47f, 65n, 66n, 74n, 77n, 112, 113f
saving 19ff, 32, 37, 43n, 47f, 74n, 75, 79, 100n

Sacrifice 11f, 39, 67f, 69ff, 83f, 86, 90, 93n, 100f, 103, 105f, 112ff, 119
Salvation, eternal, see Eternal
from enemies, see Enemies
Samaritans 2f
Security 19ff, 27ff, 32f, 38, 92n, 116f
Servant of Yahweh 1f, 42n, 54f, 66, 67, 80f, 108f, 119, 121ff
Service 18f, 24ff, 32f, 34f, 114f
Sevenfold punishment 17f, 32, (88)
Sin 18ff, 32, 34f, 36, 38f, 44, 49, 50n, 50f, 58f, 69f, 75, 79, 82, 88, 94ff, 105, 112f, 115

Sinful doubt 24ff, 32f
inclination, see Inclination
Sinfulness, universal, see Birth
Solidarity, see Corporate
Sovereignty of God, see Election
Spirit of holiness from God 10f, 19ff, 24ff, 27ff, 32ff, 39, 48n, 51f, 54ff, 63f, 77n, 84f, 89, 92f, 97f, 99, 111, 116f, 119, 121ff
Standing before God, see Communion
Suffering 37, 39, 46f, 47n, 69f, 75n, 105f, 108f, 112ff, 119f, 122f
Supererogation 1, 45, 55f, 84f, 119f

Teacher of Righteousness 4f, 6, 38, 88, 93n, 94, 103f, 116,
Teaching 17ff, 18ff, 22ff, 24ff, 27ff, 32-36, 38f, 42n, 43f, 50f, 54f, 74, 115
Textual variants at Qumran 3
Tribulation 14ff, 19, 31, 34f, 38
Trust 24ff, 32f, 36-38, (46), 51f, 116
Truth 19, 22ff, 27ff, 32f, 39, 46, 66, 74, 84f, 116f, 122f

Uncleanness 58, 66, 84f, 89f, 92f, 95f, 98f, 102f, 105, 113f, 119
Universal sinfulness, see Birth
Universalism 46f, 47n
Unworthiness 19, 32, 53, 77f

Water 27ff, 35, 58f
Weakness, human, see Pity
Wisdom 24ff, 35, 42n, 89, 93, 96, 108
Wrath of God 10f, 24ff, 32f, 36f, 39, 42f, 44, 47n, 54f, 73, 74n, 77f, 80f, 87-89, 92f, 113f, 115

Zoroastrianism 2f